SMOKING

SALMON & STEELHEAD

Scott & Tiffany Haugen

**Frank
Amato**
PORTLAND

Dedication

For the Haugen boys

Acknowledgments

We would like to thank all of the people who contributed their favorite recipes to this book. Your help allowed us to create a comprehensive work, offering a wide array of smoking options.

By assembling such a variety of unique recipes, people can now experiment to find tastes that most appeal to them, and the people with whom they share their smoked fish. Ultimately, a savored, highly appreciated end product results.

Published in 2005 by
FRANK AMATO PUBLICATIONS, INC.
PO Box 82112 • Portland, Oregon 97282
(503) 653-8108
Softbound ISBN: 1-57188-290-1
Softbound UPC: 0-81127-00119-4
Photography by Scott Haugen
Book Design: Esther Poleo Design
Printed in Hong Kong

Contents

Introduction

What you will find in these pages are workable recipes that have been time-tested in heated smokers using easy-to-find ingredients. In many cases, you'll find the handling process to be as intriguing and instrumental in deriving a specific flavor as the recipe itself.

The collection of recipes in this book, both wet and dry brines, are for smoking salmon and steelhead. When dealing with these fatty fish, the objective of a wet brine is to immerse the fillets in water and desired ingredients, whereby saturating the flesh with flavors. In dry brining, the objective is similar, but the moisture content is initially drawn out of the fish which not only enhances the essence of the meat, but slows bacterial formation as well.

The process of hot smoking fish is simple: the fats are drawn out while sealing in the flavor and juices. The combination of heat and smoke break down the fibers within the meat, while

Fully submerging fillets in a wet brine is essential for attaining a balanced flavor.

Dry brines cause a great deal of juicing to occur.

simultaneously releasing fats. The result is a tender piece of cooked meat packed with flavor. The longer the meat is exposed to heat, the drier it becomes.

No matter what recipe you apply, the goal in attaining a well-textured piece of smoked fish lies in creating a balance between salt, sugar, smoke and heat. Adding other spices and flavors you wish the meat to carry is also part of the equation. It should be noted, however, that hot smoking fish is not a form of preservation. Smoked fish has a shelf-life very similar to that of cooked fish, and if refrigerated, should not be kept much more than a week. Vacuum sealing and canning are ways to keep smoked fish for extended periods of time.

■ EXPANDING THE HORIZON

Our families have been smoking fish for many generations, and it's something we enjoy as well. Several of the recipes in this book are a direct result of our own experimentation, and many were influenced by our global travels. One aspect of smoking we enjoy, is trying to find a recipe to match our mood, the season, or the flavors we crave at the time.

When it comes to smoking fish, many people stick to their favorite recipe, not wanting to wane from what they know works. This book encourages experimentation with recipes that satisfy other tastes. One of the best ways to accomplish this is to divide up fillets into different brines and smoke them at the same time.

On a big salmon we'll often get three or four brines going at once. By placing the fish in separate brines, a range of flavors can be attained. When it comes time to air-dry the pieces, simply place

Experimenting with multiple brines is a good way to find a flavor you like. Here, Dill Infusion, Extra Hot Habeñero and Japanese Touch recipes were used on one large chinook.

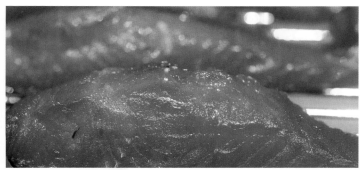

The formation of a pellicle – that glazed look fillets get when air drying after having soaked in brine – is a key step in many smoking recipes.

Brines can be altered to personal preference.

them on the smoking racks, making certain they will not drip onto one another. As the pellicle forms — the glazed layer that encases the fillets when exposed to air — juices will be sealed in the meat, so each recipe will absorb only the smoke, not the flavors of the other batches. This is a great way to add variety to your diet, and experiment with small portions of fish to see if you're happy with the final results. Of course, the more fish you have access to, the greater your level of flexibility and experimentation can be.

■ ALTER TO YOUR TASTE

One of the benefits of smoking your own fish is that you can create a flavor that appeals to your senses. Many of the recipes we've worked with over the years are quite different from their original form. When living in Alaska's Arctic, we smoked a great deal of fish, though were often limited to the ingredients on hand. As we moved to warmer climates with easy to access markets, not only did our smoking style change, but so did many of the ingredients. The result has been a collection of diverse flavors we never knew smoked fish could carry.

For this reason, we encourage you to experiment with the recipes found in this book. If you like some of the ingredients but not others, switch them around to suit your taste. If you desire more of a sweet, salty, hot or tangy flavor, adjust the recipes accordingly.

■ THE BEST SMOKING FISH

When it comes to smoking fish, there are many misconceptions as to which fish smoke best. As with cooking, the fresher the fish, the better the flavor will be. In other words, your best cooking fish is also your best smoking fish. This is because oil content is higher, the meat is firm and less gamey tasting, resulting in a quality end product that greatly accentuates the ingredients in the brine, as well as capturing the smoke flavor.

When targeting fish for the smoker, it's best to avoid the dark, beaten and battered specimens that are nearing their spawning grounds. These fish are better left to perpetuate the species, and turn out a lesser product in the smoker. While the smoke flavor can mask some of the less desirable qualities of aged fish, it will not restore the edibility to a level it once was when the fish was in better condition.

Many connoisseurs of smoked fish will even go so far as to smoke their favorite cuts, while cooking the remainder of the meat. Some of the best-tasting smoked fish comes from the bellies and collars, where oil content runs high. These cuts take longer to cook because of that oil content. If not allowed to thoroughly cook, the flesh will be mushy, and so are often dismissed as less than desirable. But left in the smoker to firm up, these oily sections are perhaps the best eating meat.

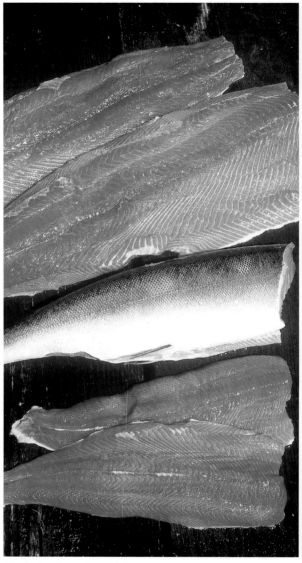

The higher the quality of fish you start with, the better taste and texture it will have in the end product.

For each recipe in this book, we have referenced the fish to be smoked as "fillets." Depending on the size fish you are preparing, fillet size will vary. The fillets cut off a 40-pound chinook will be much thicker than those from an eight-pound steelhead. The size to which fillets are trimmed will ultimately depend on your smoker's performance and the ambient conditions during the time of smoking. The more you experiment with fillets, the better suited you'll become at preparing them to meet your preference.

■ PREPARING & PROPORTIONING YOUR BRINE

In preparing any brine, it's best done in a vessel that won't transmit foul tastes. Glass, crockery or plastic containers work well, as do stainless-steel bowls. When exposed to ingredients in some brines, wood and aluminum bowls undergo a chemical reaction, whereby tainting the meat.

When it comes to brines, we are not fond of reusing them. After the slimes, fats and internal moisture leach out of an initial batch of cured meat you will not want to subject a consequent batch of fish to the brine. Rather than reuse a brine, try rationing from the outset to ensure proper proportions of a fresh brine are used each time.

When preparing any brine, note the volume of ingredients and the amount of fish you plan on smoking. Some of the brines listed in this book contain enough ingredients to prepare 50 pounds of meat, others no more than a couple pounds. **Unless otherwise noted, all recipes will easily accommodate approximately 20 pounds of fish.**

Unless specified, each recipe is for a fillet sliced two to three inches thick with the skin on. The thickness of the fillets you use will vary, as will the smoking time.

■ OPTIMIZING FLAVOR

One of our favorite ways to eat smoked fish is hot, right out of the smoker, but this is true only for select cuts. The oily belly and collar sections are delectable hot off the racks. And while other, thicker pieces are also tasty right out of the smoker, they often harbor harsh smoke flavors, especially on the surface.

If these flavors are a turnoff, remove the skin and immediately refrigerate the pieces. Keep refrigerated for a day or so, giving the meat time to reabsorb the flavors. The end result is a more moist, rich and succulently flavored fish that best represents the ingredients that went into creating it.

Salmon and steelhead acquire smoke flavors quite quickly. Smoke flavors can be optimized by burning more chips during the cooking process. In addition, by preheating the smoker and getting the chips burning prior to placing the fish in the unit, a more intense smoke flavor will be delivered early in the smoking process.

You may find that a few recipes are fairly similar in terms of ingredients, however, the handling processes are quite different, resulting in a different tasting end product. You'll discover that handling processes play a major role in optimizing and capturing specific flavors in your smoked fish.

■ KNOW YOUR SMOKER

Ultimately, the best smoked fish will be achieved through practice. Unfortunately, that means a lot of trial and error. By experimenting with different recipes and learning the parameters of your smoker, what it's capable of doing, how it performs in varied climatic conditions and even seasons of the year, you'll gain the most knowledge of the overall smoking process.

When we lived in Alaska's Arctic, we often smoked fish in 50° below zero temperatures. Even with our Little Chief smoker wrapped in a heat blanket, the process took 10-12 hours, and saw us going through several pans of chips, in an effort to generate more heat. Due to the extreme cold, the meat typically had to be finished in the oven. When using the same smoker while living in Indonesia, the cooking time dramatically decreased. Now that we live in Oregon, our cooking times vary with the changing seasons. By knowing how your smoker reacts and performs in the environment in which you live, you will be able to turn out a quality product every time. These are points you might want to record and keep track of for future reference.

There are many styles and brands of smokers on the market, and what you get depends on personal preference. Some depend on a smoker with built-in temperature gauges and control valves, while a select few constructed their own smokers.

The recipes found in these pages can be applied by anyone, no matter what style smoker you use. No matter what smoker you prefer, be sure to always place it in a well-ventilated area, away from walls. Do not use smokers on wood floors or decks and be certain all connections — be they gas or electrical — are solid and in place.

By preparing yourself with basic ingredients, quality fish and an open mind, the world of smoking salmon and steelhead can be unlike anything ever imagined. Capturing unique flavors in your smoked fish is simple, and once you discover how delectable and truly diverse they can be, the only question you'll have is, why didn't I start doing this earlier?

Wet Brines

■ Jerry Haugen with a hefty Kenai River king salmon.

Always found on a tattered piece of paper stuck to the refrigerator, this recipe was passed down several generations, and is still a favorite in the Haugen household.

Instructions:

1. Mix the ingredients in a large bowl with a wire whisk until sugar is dissolved.

2. Add enough pepper to "gray" the water or to your taste.

3. Submerge fish in brine skin side down on the bottom layer, meat side down on the next layer. Repeat layering skin to skin, meat to meat.

4. Place a weighted plate on top of the fish to fully submerge fillets.

5. Soak fish in brine 3 1/2 hours.

6. Place on racks and air dry 2-4 hours, or until a firm pellicle forms.

7. Smoke 5 to 8 hours, depending on volume of meat and outside temperature.

Ingredients:

■ 1 1/2 quarts water
■ 2/3 cup Morton's Tender Quick
■ 3/4 cup white sugar
■ 1/4 cup brown sugar
■ 3 teaspoons liquid hickory smoke
■ 3 teaspoons liquid garlic
■ Black pepper to taste

Notes:

This recipe adapts well to many different chip types.

Herb Medley

A favorite in the summer when the herb garden is full. Any fresh herbs can be used, just experiment to your liking.

Ingredients:

- 1 quart water
- 1/2 cup Morton's Tender Quick
- 3/4 cup white sugar
- 1/3 cup fresh parsley
- 3-4 sprigs fresh rosemary
- 1/3 cup fresh basil
- 3-5 sprigs fresh dill
- 3 teaspoons white pepper
- 8 cloves garlic, crushed

Instructions:

1. Rinse herbs and tear into small pieces.
2. Mix all ingredients in a large bowl with a wire whisk until sugar is dissolved.
3. Submerge bottom layer of fish in brine skin side down, then meat side down on the next layer. Repeat layering skin to skin, meat to meat.
4. Place a weighted plate on top of the fish to fully submerge all fillets.
5. Soak fish in brine 3-5 hours, the longer it soaks, the more intense the flavor.
6. Place on racks and air dry until pellicle is formed, 1-3 hours.
7. Smoke to desired texture. Cooking time varies from 3-10 hours, depending on the smoker, volume of fish and outdoor conditions. Check frequently, do not overcook.

Notes:

Fresh herbal flavor throughout, nice glaze. A dark, rich finished product.

One of the greatest guys in the world to fish with, Bob Cobb is becoming a legendary guide on Oregon's famed Umpqua River. His smoked salmon is also making a lasting impression on those who taste it.

Instructions:

1. Mix the water, sugar, salt, soy sauce and wine in a large bowl until sugar has dissolved.
2. Soak the fish in brine, refrigerated, 12-24 hours.
3. Place fish on racks and sprinkle desired amount of onion powder, garlic powder, black pepper and Tabasco sauce.
3. Dry on racks in the refrigerator 12 hours.
4. Smoke 7 hours, changing chips every 2 hours.

Ingredients:

- 5 cups water
- 1 cup sugar
- 3/4 cup non-iodized salt
- 4 cups soy sauce
- 3 cups wine
- Onion powder
- Garlic powder
- Black pepper
- Tabasco sauce

Zesty Wine

Fenugreek, dill, coriander, ginger, allspice and bay leaves are just some of the unique ingredients in pickling spice that blend together to make this smoked fish the topic of conversation at any gathering.

Ingredients:

- 4 cups water
- 1/2 cup Morton's Tender Quick
- 2 1/2 cups white wine
- 1 cup brown sugar
- 1 tablespoon garlic powder
- 1 tablespoon onion powder
- 3 tablespoons pickling spices

Instructions:

1. Mix the ingredients in a large bowl with a wire whisk until sugar is dissolved.
2. Submerge fish in brine skin side down, then meat side down on the next layer. Repeat layering skin to skin, meat to meat.
3. Place a weighted plate on top of the fish to fully submerge fillets.
4. Soak fish in brine 5-10 hours, the longer it soaks, the more intense the flavor.
5. Place on racks and air dry until pellicle is formed, 1-3 hours.
6. Smoke to desired texture. Cooking time varies from 3-10 hours, depending on the smoker, volume of fish being smoked and outdoor conditions. Check frequently so as not to overcook.

Notes:

Good for Italian feast, an antipasto plate, hot pasta or pasta salads; assorted olives and cheeses also go well.

■ Buzz Ramsey is pleased with this Columbia River coho.

One of the world's most renowned salmon and steelhead anglers, fishing legend, Buzz Ramsey, performs wonders on the water and in the smoker.

Instructions:

1. Mix water, salt and sugar in a large bowl until sugar has dissolved.
2. Soak fish in brine overnight in the refrigerator.
3. Rinse well and pat dry with paper towels.
4. Air dry for 1 hour.
5. Place fish on racks and sprinkle with onion salt, garlic salt and black pepper.
6. Sprinkle with a final covering of sugar from a salt shaker.
7. Smoke with hickory, alder, apple or cherry wood (no more than two or three pans full) for 8 to 14 hours depending on outside temperature, how full your smoker is, and the amount of salmon fillets in the smoker.

Ingredients:

- 1 quart water
- 1/2 cup non-iodized salt
- 1 cup sugar
- Onion salt
- Garlic salt
- Black pepper
- Sugar

Notes:

The best smoking fish are spring chinook bellies and collars, but leave these cuts in the smoker longer than other portions, as they cook slower.

Sweet Teriyaki

A more traditional recipe, the molasses brings out a complex sweetness that is not overpowering.

Ingredients:

- 1 1/2 quarts water
- 1/2 cup Morton's Tender Quick
- 2/3 cup molasses
- 2 cups brown sugar
- 2 cups teriyaki sauce
- Chips

Instructions:

1. Mix the ingredients in a large bowl with a wire whisk until sugar is dissolved.
2. Submerge fish in brine skin side down on the bottom layer, meat side down on the next layer. Repeat layering skin to skin, meat to meat.
3. Place a weighted plate on top of the fish to fully submerge all fillets.
4. Soak fish in brine 4 hours.
5. Place on racks and air dry until pellicle is formed, 1-3 hours.
6. Smoke to desired texture. Cooking time varies from 3-10 hours, depending on the smoker, volume of fish being smoked and outdoor conditions. Check frequently so as not to overcook.

Notes:

Good for full-flavored, ocean-caught fish with high oil content; sweet throughout, picks up flavor of hickory chips well.

Known affectionately as the "Jig-Man," guide, Bret Stuart, has hit a home run with his steelhead jigs and this fine recipe.

Instructions:

1. Mix the ingredients in a large bowl until sugar is dissolved.
2. Soak the fish in brine 6-8 hours.
3. Dry on racks until pellicle forms.
4. Smoke until done.

Ingredients:

- 2 quarts water
- 10 ounces apple juice
- 3/4 cup non-iodized salt
- 3/4 cup white sugar
- 3/4 cup brown sugar

Notes:

Use apple-flavored chips to enhance the sweet taste given off by the apple juice. Cut down on water and add more apple juice for a stronger apple sweetness.

Blackberry Blast

A fun recipe to make during the height of blackberry season, but one that works equally well using frozen berries.

Ingredients:

- 5 cups water
- 2/3 cup Morton's Tender Quick
- 1 cup red wine
- 1 cup brown sugar
- 1 cup blackberries, crushed
- 1 cup blackberry syrup, recipe follows

Instructions:

1. Mix the ingredients in a large bowl with a wire whisk until sugar is dissolved.
2. Submerge fish in brine skin side down on the bottom layer, meat side down on the next layer. Repeat layering skin to skin, meat to meat.
3. Place a weighted plate on top of the fish to fully submerge all fillets.
4. Soak fish in brine 3-6 hours.
5. Place on racks and air dry until pellicle is formed, 1-3 hours.
6. Smoke to desired texture. Cooking time varies from 3-10 hours, depending on the smoker, volume of fish being smoked and outdoor conditions. Check frequently so as not to overcook.

Blackberry Syrup:

- 2 gallons blackberries
- 7 cups sugar

Run blackberries through a sieve to remove seeds. In a large stock pot, cook berries down to approximately 4 cups of puree. Add sugar and cook over medium heat until sugar is dissolved. Unless you plan to use the blackberry syrup within a week, you will need to can it. Put blackberry syrup in clean canning jars, adjust lids and give them a 10-15 minute bath in boiling water.

Notes:

Lightly sweet with a strong taste of blackberry. For a shortcut, use store-bought blackberry or boysenberry syrup.

The culinary delights of India are easy to recreate with the right spices. Though we don't use traditional cow dung as our source of smoke fuel, this recipe always takes us back to our safari through Corbett National Park in Northern India.

Instructions:

1. Mix the ingredients in a large bowl with a wire whisk until sugar is dissolved.
2. Submerge fish in brine skin side down on the bottom layer, meat side down on the next layer. Repeat layering skin to skin, meat to meat.
3. Place a weighted plate on top of the fish to fully submerge all fillets.
4. Soak fish in brine 3-5 hours.
5. Place on racks and air dry until pellicle is formed, 1-3 hours.
6. Smoke to desired texture. Cooking time varies from 3-10 hours, depending on the smoker, volume of fish being smoked and outdoor conditions. Check frequently so as not to overcook.

Ingredients:

- 2 quarts water
- 4 black tea bags (steep in 1 cup hot water overnight)
- 3/4 cup Morton's Tender Quick
- 1 1/3 cup brown sugar
- 1/2 teaspoon mace
- 1/2 teaspoon turmeric
- 1/2 teaspoon thyme
- 1/2 teaspoon nutmeg
- 1/2 teaspoon coriander
- 1 teaspoon fennel
- 1 teaspoon mustard seeds
- 10 green cardamom pods
- 15 whole cloves
- 10 whole allspice
- 3 cinnamon sticks

Notes:

For a more intense spice flavor, grind the spices with a mortar and pestle before putting them in the brine.

Molasses Drizzle

Long-time Alaskan resident, serious outdoorsman, and good friend Art Peck is a perfectionist in all that he does, including catching and smoking fish.

Ingredients:

- Brown sugar
- Molasses
- Non-iodized salt
- Black pepper (optional)

Instructions:

1. In a large stainless-steel or glass bowl, sprinkle a layer of brown sugar in the bottom.
2. Place 1 layer of fish, skin side down, over the brown sugar.
3. Cover with another layer of brown sugar, sprinkle a layer of salt and apply a light drizzle of molasses that covers 50% of the fish.
4. Keep layering, skin to skin, meat to meat, with brown sugar, salt and molasses.
5. Cover with cold water.
6. Soak fish in brine 1 1/2 hours.
7. Remove fish and rinse quickly under cold water, meat will be decidedly firm.
8. Place on racks. (For added sweetness, sprinkle a light dusting of brown sugar over the fish at this time.)
9. Air dry until pellicle forms, this can take up to 6 hours, depending on temperature and humidity. A circulating fan can help speed up the process.
10. Smoke until done, 4-14 hours depending on the weather and fish thickness.
11. Finish smoking process in the oven if desired.

Notes:

Recipe variations include: dill infusion (place 3 teaspoons of dry dill in a cheesecloth pouch, steep in 2 cups boiling water 30 minutes and add to water brine); add peppers of choice to spice and make recipe hotter if desired; sprinkle cumin on chips as they smoke.

Essentially a wet brine with a rub placed on the fish prior to smoking, this recipe creates a sweet, tangy flavor.

Instructions:

1. Zest lemons and limes.

2. Mix zest with brown sugar and freshly ground black pepper, set aside.

3. Mix the remaining ingredients in a large bowl with a wire whisk until sugar is dissolved.

4. Submerge fish in brine skin side down on the bottom layer, meat side down on the next layer. Repeat layering skin to skin, meat to meat.

5. Place a weighted plate on top of the fish to fully submerge all fillets.

6. Soak fish in brine 1 to 1½ hours. Do not oversoak as citric acids begin to "cook" the fish.

7. Place on racks and gently rub in the zest, sugar and pepper mixture.

8. Smoke to desired texture. Cooking time varies from 3-10 hours, depending on the smoker, volume of fish being smoked and outdoor conditions. Check frequently so as not to overcook.

Ingredients:

- 5 cups water
- 1/2 cup lemon juice
- 1/2 cup lime juice
- 1/4 cup light corn syrup
- 1/2 cup non-iodized salt

RUB:

- Zest from 2 lemons
- Zest from 2 limes
- 1/2 cup brown sugar
- 1 tablespoon freshly ground black pepper

Notes:

Excellent sweet, lemony taste, a favorite of many who' ve tried it.

Hint of Apple

An avid angler, Art Martin has gone to great pains to perfect his brine. Because this recipe accommodates a 16-quart container full of salmon or steelhead fillets, it's a great one to use on those days you've tagged out.

Ingredients:

- 64 ounces frozen apple juice concentrate (do not add water)
- 4 pounds brown sugar
- 1/2 cup non-iodized salt
- 28 ounces Yoshida's original gourmet sauce
- 2 large sweet onions, diced
- 4 tablespoons garlic, minced
- 1/2 tablespoon Worcestershire sauce
- 1-2 teaspoons liquid smoke
- 1 teaspoon fresh ground black pepper

Instructions:

1. Mix ingredients in a 4-gallon, non-aluminum container making sure to fully dissolve salt and brown sugar.
2. Score thicker fillets on flesh side every 2 inches to ensure proper absorption of brine.
3. Submerge fillets in brine, placing top layer skin side up.
4. Brine in refrigerator 24-48 hours, stirring fillets every six hours.
5. Smoke 4-8 hours depending on thickness. Place thinner pieces away from the heat source, thicker pieces closer to heat source.
6. Use up to 3 pans of apple or cherry hardwood chips.
7. Check often and remove thinner pieces first to ensure fillets do not get overly dry.

Notes:

With the exception of the salt, you can adjust the ingredients to taste.

One of our favorite recipes, a sweet, strong flavor is what you'll discover when sinking your teeth into this scrumptious fish.

Instructions:

1. Mix the ingredients in a large bowl with a wire whisk until sugar is dissolved.

2. Submerge fish in brine skin side down on the bottom layer, meat side down on the next layer. Repeat layering skin to skin, meat to meat.

3. Place a weighted plate on top of the fish to fully submerge all meat.

4. Soak fish in brine 3-4 hours.

5. Smoke to desired texture. Cooking time varies from 3-10 hours, depending on the smoker, volume of fish being smoked and outdoor conditions. Check frequently so as not to overcook.

Ingredients:

- 1 quart water
- 1 cup apple juice
- 1 cup brandy
- 1 cup soy sauce
- 1/4 cup rock salt
- 3/4 cup brown sugar
- 2 teaspoons granulated garlic
- 2 teaspoons granulated onion
- 1 teaspoon fresh ground black pepper
- 15 whole cloves

Notes:

Soak chips, alder or hickory, in brandy for 10 minutes before smoking.

Tropical Tang

On the sweeter side, this recipe also yields a nice, moist product. Water can be cut down and additional juice added for an even deeper citrus flavor.

Ingredients:

- 1 1/2 quarts water
- 2/3 cup non-iodized salt
- 1/2 cup white sugar
- 1/2 cup brown sugar
- 2 cups crushed pineapple with juice
- Zest of 1 orange
- 1 orange, peeled and chopped

Instructions:

1. Mix the ingredients in a large bowl with a wire whisk until sugar is dissolved.
2. Submerge fish in brine skin side down on the bottom layer, meat side down on the next layer. Repeat layering skin to skin, meat to meat.
3. Place a weighted plate on top of the fish to fully submerge all fillets.
4. Soak fish in brine 6-8 hours, the longer it soaks, the sweeter the flavor.
5. Place on racks and air dry until pellicle is formed, 1-3 hours.
6. Sprinkle fish with a light dusting of white or brown sugar.
7. Smoke to desired texture. Cooking time varies from 3-10 hours, depending on the smoker, volume of fish being smoked and outdoor conditions. Check frequently so as not to overcook.

Notes:
Works well with hickory or apple wood chips

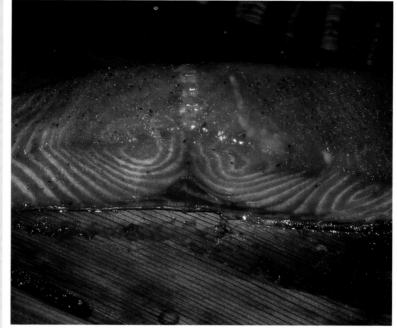

Professional hunting and fishing guide Skip Geer is a man who spends more time afield in a year than most guys do in a decade. Skip brings this recipe to camp in a sealed plastic baggy, where he can either cook or smoke the fish.

Instructions:

1. Mix the ingredients in a large bowl.
2. Submerge fish in brine skin side down on the bottom layer, meat side down on the next layer. Repeat layering skin to skin, meat to meat.
3. Place a weighted plate on top of the fish to fully submerge all fillets.
4. Soak fish in brine overnight.
5. Place on racks and air dry until pellicle is formed, about 1 hour.
6. Smoke to desired texture. Cooking time varies from 3-10 hours, depending on the smoker, volume of fish being smoked and outdoor conditions. Check frequently so as not to overcook.

Ingredients:

- 1 cup real maple syrup
- 1 cup Yoshida's original gourmet sauce
- 1/2 cup sweet BBQ sauce

Notes:

This versatile brine/marinade makes an outstanding plank-cooked fish. Brine will cure up to 10 pounds of fish.

Hot Pepper

For those who like a little "fire" in their smoked fish, the ratio of ingredients in this recipe can be altered to meet anyone's taste.

Ingredients:

- 7 cups water
- 1 cup corn syrup
- 3/4 cup non-iodized salt
- 2 tablespoons red pepper flakes
- 3-6 teaspoons Tabasco Sauce
- 2 teaspoons liquid garlic
- 1 teaspoon garlic salt

Instructions:

1. Mix the ingredients in a large bowl with a wire whisk until sugar is dissolved.
2. Submerge fish in brine skin side down on the bottom layer, meat side down on the next layer. Repeat layering skin to skin, meat to meat.
3. Place a weighted plate on top of the fish to fully submerge all fillets.
4. Soak fish in brine 2-3 hours.
5. For an extra spicy fish, additional red pepper flakes can be sprinkled on the fish. Tabasco, or any other hot pepper sauce, can also be sprayed on the fish at this time to even further enhance the surface flavor.
6. Place on racks and air dry until pellicle is formed, 1-3 hours.
7. Smoke to desired texture. Cooking time varies from 3-10 hours, depending on the smoker, volume of fish being smoked and outdoor conditions. Check frequently so as not to overcook.

Notes:

Serve with Tabasco or other hot pepper sauce as some may like to add even more fire.

With its strong smoke flavor, this recipe works especially well when making dips or appetizers using smoked fish.

Instructions:

1. Mix the ingredients in a large bowl with a wire whisk until sugar is dissolved.

2. Submerge fish in brine skin side down on the bottom layer, meat side down on the next layer. Repeat layering skin to skin, meat to meat.

3. Place a weighted plate on top of the fish to fully submerge all meat.

4. Soak fish in brine 3½ to 4 hours.

5. Place on racks and air dry until pellicle is formed, 1-3 hours.

6. Smoke to desired texture. Cooking time varies from 3-10 hours, depending on the smoker, volume of fish being smoked and outdoor conditions. Check frequently so as not to overcook.

Ingredients:

- 1 1/2 quarts water
- 2/3 cup Morton's Tender Quick
- 1/2 cup brown sugar
- 1/2 cup white sugar
- 4 teaspoons mesquite liquid smoke flavoring
- 3 teaspoons garlic juice
- 2 teaspoons black pepper

Notes:

Use mesquite chips for the most intense flavor.

Taste of Lemon

Living where salmon and steelhead can be caught five minutes from their doorstep every day of the year, Bob Cobb and his wife Peggy have plenty of opportunities to experiment with smoking recipes. This is another of their favorites.

Ingredients:

- 1 1/2 gallons water
- 2 cups rock salt
- 1 cup dark brown sugar
- 6 tablespoons garlic powder
- 1 lemon
- 1 tablespoon lemon pepper

Instructions:

1. Mix the water, rock salt, brown sugar and garlic powder in a large bowl until sugar is dissolved.

2. Soak the fish, refrigerated, in the brine 6-12 hours.

3. Rinse surface salt.

4. Dry overnight on racks in the refrigerator.

5. Sprinkle a few drops of fresh-squeezed lemon and lemon pepper on each piece of fish.

6. Smoke 5-8 hours, using 5-8 pans of chips.

7. If not completely done in the smoker, finish in the oven at 300° for 20 minutes.

While living in Indonesia, we developed a love for the combination of sesame and ginger. Together these tastes complement smoked fish, bringing out a savory, delicious flavor.

Instructions:

1. Mix the ingredients in a large bowl with a wire whisk until sugar is dissolved.

2. Submerge fish in brine skin side down on the bottom layer, meat side down on the next layer. Repeat layering skin to skin, meat to meat.

3. Place a weighted plate on top of the fish to fully submerge all meat.

4. Soak fish in brine 2 hours.

5. Place on racks and air dry until pellicle is formed, 1-3 hours.

6. Smoke to desired texture. Cooking time varies from 3-10 hours, depending on the smoker, volume of fish being smoked and outdoor conditions. Check frequently so as not to overcook.

Ingredients:

- 1 1/2 quarts water
- 1/2 cup brown sugar
- 1/2 cup white sugar
- 1/2 cup non-iodized salt
- 2 tablespoons sesame oil
- 1/3 cup soy sauce
- 1/3 cup rice vinegar
- 1/2 cup roasted sesame seeds
- 2 teaspoons garlic juice
- 3 tablespoons fresh ginger, sliced

Notes:
The sesame oil helps fish pick up a hardy smoke flavor. Choose alder or hickory chips for smoking.

Mustard-Rum

A light-tasting smoked fish that captures the complexity of many flavors.

Ingredients:

- 1 1/2 quarts water
- 3/4 cup brown sugar
- 3/4 cup white sugar
- 1/2 cup non-iodized salt
- 1/3 cup Worcestershire sauce
- 2 teaspoons liquid garlic juice
- 2 tablespoons dry mustard
- 1/2 cup rum

Instructions:

1. Mix the ingredients in a large bowl with a wire whisk until sugar is dissolved.

2. Submerge fish in brine skin side down on the bottom layer, meat side down on the next layer. Repeat layering skin to skin, meat to meat.

3. Place a weighted plate on top of the fish to fully submerge all fillets.

4. Soak fish in brine 3 hours.

5. Place on racks and air dry until pellicle is formed, 1-3 hours.

6. Smoke to desired texture. Cooking time varies from 3-10 hours, depending on the smoker, volume of fish being smoked and outdoor conditions. Check frequently so as not to overcook.

Avid angler and active member of the Eugene chapter of the Northwest Steelheaders, Bruce Bashor's favorite recipe is one he attained from good friend and noted angler Woody Bonde.

Instructions:

1. Mix all ingredients in a large crock.
2. Soak fish in brine 12 hours in refrigerator.
3. Place fish skin side down on a clean cotton bath towel and pat meat side dry with paper towels.
4. Let pellicle form, 45 minutes to 1 hour.
5. Place fish on racks and start up smoker.
6. Put the fish in the smoker when the first pan of chips starts to smoke.
7. Use 2-3 pans of apple wood chips.
8. Check small pieces at 5 hours, larger pieces take about 8 hours.
9. Remove fish from smoker and cool.
10. Place in a bowl and cover with plastic wrap.
11. Refrigerate overnight and it's ready to eat.

Ingredients:

- 4 cups water
- 2 cups soy sauce
- 2 cups 100% pure apple juice
- 1/3 cup non-iodized salt
- 1 cup brown sugar
- 1 teaspoon garlic salt
- 1 teaspoon onion salt
- 1 teaspoon black pepper

Notes:
Robust smokey flavor, mildly sweet, tasting almost like candy.

Saucy Smoked

Those who like the sweet tang of barbecue with a dominating smoke flavor will love this version of smoked salmon or steelhead.

Ingredients:

- 1 1/2 quarts water
- 1/2 cup Morton's Tender Quick
- 1 cup brown sugar
- 10 ounces of your favorite steak sauce
- Freshly ground black pepper

Instructions:

1. Mix the ingredients in a large bowl with a wire whisk until sugar is dissolved.
2. Submerge fish in brine skin side down on the bottom layer, meat side down on the next layer. Repeat layering skin to skin, meat to meat.
3. Place a weighted plate on top of the fish to fully submerge all fillets.
4. Soak fish in brine 2-3 hours. The longer it soaks, the more intense the flavor.
5. Place on racks and grind pepper on top of fish while still moist.
5. Air dry until pellicle is formed, 1-3 hours.
6. Smoke to desired texture. Cooking time varies from 3-10 hours, depending on the smoker, volume of fish being smoked and outdoor conditions. Check frequently so as not to overcook.

Notes:

Use as many pans of chips as desired as this recipe holds the flavor well. Mesquite and cherry wood chips are a favorite.

The balanced combination of thyme, oregano, savory, marjoram, basil, rosemary and sage in Italian seasoning blend well, making this recipe a favorite with other Italian dishes.

Instructions:

1. Mix the ingredients in a large bowl with a wire whisk until sugar is dissolved.

2. Submerge fish in brine skin side down on the bottom layer, meat side down on the next layer. Repeat layering skin to skin, meat to meat.

3. Place a weighted plate on top of the fish to fully submerge all meat.

4. Soak fish in brine 2-3 hours.

5. Lightly rinse fish to remove most of the seasonings. Some is desirable but too much may become charred in the smoking process.

6. Place on racks and air dry until pellicle is formed, 1-3 hours.

7. Smoke to desired texture. Cooking time varies from 3-10 hours, depending on the smoker, volume of fish being smoked and outdoor conditions. Check frequently so as not to overcook.

Ingredients:

- 1 1/2 quarts water
- 1 cup white sugar
- 1/2 cup non-iodized salt
- 1 cup red or white wine
- 3 tablespoons minced garlic
- 1 tablespoon granulated onion
- 8 tablespoons Italian seasoning
- 2 teaspoons freshly ground black pepper

Notes:

Using red wine makes a darker colored final product. Perfect with any antipasto dish.

Patrick Roelle, of Fishpatrick's Guide Service, is a hard-working, talented individual who credits the outcome of this recipe to the handling process.

Ingredients:

- 1/2 pound brown sugar
- 1 palm (hand) full chopped or minced garlic
- 2 cups soy sauce
- 1/2 cup white wine, optional
- Kosher salt
- Black pepper

Instructions:

1. Mix sugar, garlic, soy sauce and wine in a large bowl.
2. Place fish on brine, skin side up.
3. Cover fish with plastic wrap. Push around and into pan to seal out air and force fish into the brine.
4. Let soak 12 hours, refrigerated.
5. Remove cover, mix fish well, recover and leave for another 12 hours, refrigerated.
6. Remove fish from brine and rinse under cold water.
7. Place fish on racks, skin side down.
8. Sprinkle Kosher salt and freshly ground black pepper on each piece.
9. Allow to glaze in the wind 1 hour.
10. Smoke until done.
11. Use 3 pans of large chunky alder chips in a smoker.
12. Serve right away with rice and a vegetable, or
13. Remove from smoker and place onto a large plate, with a little space between each piece.
14. Place in refrigerator, uncovered, 24 hours.
15. Add additional salt if desired.

Notes:

Variations of this recipe include adding fresh ginger to the brine, substituting Yoshida's gourmet sauce or teriyaki sauce for the soy sauce, adding more or less brown sugar to taste. Brine will cure up to 10 pounds of fish.

The tastes of honey, lime and garlic infuse the fish with a distinct tropical flavor.

Instructions:

1. Mix the ingredients in a large bowl.
2. Submerge fish in brine skin side down on the bottom layer, meat side down on the next layer. Repeat layering skin to skin, meat to meat.
3. Place a weighted plate on top of the fish to fully submerge all fillets.
4. Soak fish in brine 1 1/2-2 hours. Do not oversoak as citric acids begin to "cook" the fish.
5. Place fish on racks and garlic slices on top of fish.
6. Smoke to desired texture. Cooking time varies from 3-10 hours, depending on the smoker, volume of fish being smoked and outdoor conditions. Check frequently so as not to overcook.

Ingredients:

- 1 1/2 quarts water
- 1/2 cup lime juice
- 1 cup honey
- 3/4 cup Morton's Tender Quick
- 5 cloves garlic, thinly sliced
- Zest of 1 lime
- 1 teaspoon liquid smoke
- 2 teaspoons finely ground white pepper

Notes:

Smoked garlic on top of the fish is an added bonus for true garlic lovers.

Sugared Tequila

Fans of tequila should try this recipe. Due to the misting of the alcohol, the flavor of tequila shows through in the final product. Just don't smoke the worm!

Ingredients:

- 5 cups water
- 3/4 cup rock salt
- 1 cup tequila
- 1 cup brown sugar
- 2 limes, thinly sliced
- 1 tablespoon garlic, minced or sliced
- 2 teaspoons white pepper
- Additional tequila for spray bottle
- White sugar for sprinkling

Instructions:

1. Mix the ingredients in a large bowl with a wire whisk until sugar is dissolved.

2. Submerge fish in brine skin side down on the bottom layer, meat side down on the next layer. Repeat layering skin to skin, meat to meat.

3. Place a weighted plate on top of the fish to fully submerge all fillets.

4. Soak fish in brine 3-4 hours.

5. Generously spray the fish with tequila and sprinkle a layer of white sugar on top.

6. Smoke to desired texture. Cooking time varies from 3-10 hours, depending on the smoker, volume of fish being smoked and outdoor conditions. Check frequently so as not to overcook.

Longtime friend and avid angler, Matt Haugen delivers more than just a good smoking recipe; as a top obstetrician, he also brought our two sons into this world.

Instructions:

1. Mix the ingredients in a large saucepan.
2. Bring mixture to a boil for 15 minutes, cool to room temperature (or keep in the refrigerator until the following day).
3. Soak fresh fish in brine 4 hours. Soak previously frozen fish in brine 2 hours.
4. Rinse fish in cold water, blot with paper towels.
5. Place on racks and air dry with a fan.
6. Smoke to desired texture. Cooking time varies from 3-10 hours, depending on the smoker, volume of fish being smoked and outdoor conditions. Check frequently so as not to overcook.

Ingredients:

- 4 cups water
- 2 cups apple juice
- 1/2 cup pickling salt
- 1/2 cup light soy sauce
- 1 cup brown sugar
- 1/4 cup maple syrup
- 6 bay leaves
- 1 clove garlic
- 1 teaspoon allspice
- 1/4 teaspoon pepper

Notes:
Mild sweet taste, goes well in a dip or spread. Use alder or apple chips.

Chinese 5-Spice

Cinnamon, cloves, fennel, anise and ginger combine sweet, warm, cool and spicy flavors to make an intense spice-blend that adds a distinctly Asian flavor to smoked fish.

Ingredients:

- 1 1/2 quarts water
- 1/2 cup Morton's Tender Quick
- 2 tablespoons Chinese 5-spice
- 1/3 cup oyster sauce
- 1/3 cup soy sauce
- 1 cup white sugar
- 1/4 cup rice vinegar

Instructions:

1. Mix the ingredients in a large bowl with a wire whisk until sugar is dissolved.
2. Submerge fish in brine skin side down on the bottom layer, meat side down on the next layer. Repeat layering skin to skin, meat to meat.
3. Place a weighted plate on top of the fish to fully submerge all fillets.
4. Soak fish in brine 3½ hours.
5. Place on racks and air dry until pellicle is formed, 1-3 hours.
6. Smoke to desired texture. Cooking time varies from 3-10 hours, depending on the smoker, volume of fish being smoked and outdoor conditions. Check frequently so as not to overcook.

Notes:

With a more savory than sweet smoked taste, this versatile recipe lends itself well to different dips. pictured above, honey-mustard and sweet chili-sauce with mayonnaise.

Extra Hot Habañero

Looking to add a little fire to your smoked fish? The petite habañero chili is the way to go.

Instructions:

1. Mix the ingredients, include chili seeds, in a large bowl with a wire whisk until sugar is dissolved.
2. Score fish lightly if a hot flavor is desired throughout.
3. Submerge fish in brine skin side down on the bottom layer, meat side down on the next layer. Repeat layering skin to skin, meat to meat.
4. Place a weighted plate on top of the fish to fully submerge all fillets.
5. Soak fish in brine 3-4 hours.
6. Place fish on racks, spray with Tabasco or other hot pepper spray if desired.
7. Place on racks and air dry until pellicle is formed, 1-3 hours.
8. Smoke to desired texture. Cooking time varies from 3-10 hours, depending on the smoker, volume of fish being smoked and outdoor conditions. Check frequently so as not to overcook.
9. Once fish has cooled, remove from racks, place in an airtight container and refrigerate overnight.

Ingredients:

- 1 1/2 quarts water
- 3/4 cup Morton's Tender Quick
- 1 cup brown sugar
- 1/2 cup white sugar
- 6 habañero chilies, thinly sliced
- 3 jalapeño chilies, thinly sliced
- 1 tablespoon red pepper flakes
- 1/4 teaspoon red food coloring
- 2 teaspoons liquid garlic
- 1 tablespoon seasoned pepper blend
- Spray with Tabasco, optional

Notes:

Not as hot a flavor as would be expected, but a nice sharp taste highlighting the smoke. Use rubber gloves when handling peppers.

Subtly Soy

Dennis Jarvi uses his own alder wood chunks, combining them with prepared chips, to enhance the flavor in this skinless smoke recipe. This is one Dennis and his wife have modified over the years to fit their taste.

Ingredients:

- 1 cup soy sauce
- 2 cups brown sugar
- 2 tablespoons garlic
- 1 tablespoon basil
- 2 tablespoons dill
- 1 cup white wine

Instructions:

1. Mix ingredients in a large bowl.
2. Cut fish pieces from fillets in 3/4"-thick strips, removing skin and fat.
3. Soak fish in brine 15-18 hours in refrigerator.
4. Drain on paper towels and blot dry.
5. Place on oiled racks in smoker.
6. Smoke 5-7 hours or until done.
7. Let cool, place in an airtight container in the refrigerator for a few days to let things mingle.
8. Eat right away or vacuum seal to prolong freshness.

Notes:

Overall texture is firm, not dry, chewy but not tough. Relatively sweet with a nice fish flavor. Brine will cure up to 10 pounds of fish.

A fun recipe to make when raspberries are in season, this one works equally well using frozen raspberry puree.

Instructions:

1. Mix the ingredients in a large bowl with a wire whisk until sugar is dissolved.

2. Submerge fish in brine skin side down on the bottom layer, meat side down on the next layer. Repeat layering skin to skin, meat to meat.

3. Place a weighted plate on top of the fish to fully submerge all fillets.

4. Soak fish in brine 3 1/2 hours.

5. Place on racks and air dry until pellicle is formed, 1-3 hours.

6. Smoke to desired texture. Cooking time varies from 3-10 hours, depending on the smoker, volume of fish being smoked and outdoor conditions. Check frequently so as not to overcook.

Ingredients:

- 1 quart water
- 2 cups raspberry puree
- 1/2 cup Morton's Tender Quick
- 1/2 cup real maple syrup
- 2/3 cup brown sugar
- 1 tablespoon coriander
- 1 cup white wine vinegar

Notes:

A smooth, mild recipe that takes on the flavors of the smoke. Apple wood chips are recommended.

Family Secret

Carl Campbell grew up in Fossil, Oregon and works as a part-time guide for Mah-Hah Outfitters. He and his family worked hard to developed this recipe, one they were a bit reluctant to part with. This recipe was brought to our attention by noted guide and good friend Steve Fleming, owner and operator of Mah-Hah Outfitters.

Ingredients:

- 2 cups water
- 1 cup apple juice
- 1/4 cup Morton's Tender Quick
- 1/2 cup brown sugar
- 1/2 teaspoon onion salt
- 1/2 teaspoon garlic salt
- 4 squirts Tabasco sauce
- A palm (hand) full of crushed red peppers

Instructions:

1. Mix ingredients in gallon jar of water.
2. Submerge fish in brine skin side down on the bottom layer, meat side down on the next layer. Repeat layering skin to skin, meat to meat.
3. Soak fish in brine 6 hours.
4. Place fish on racks until glazed.
5. Smoke until done. If it does not get done in smoker, finish in a food dehydrator.

Notes:

Brine will cure up to 10 pounds of fish. Recommended wood chips: alder.

A nice, light recipe that is a must-try if you enjoy exotic flavors.

Instructions:

1. Mix the ingredients in a large bowl with a wire whisk until sugar is dissolved.

2. Submerge fish in brine skin side down on the bottom layer, meat side down on the next layer. Repeat layering skin to skin, meat to meat.

3. Place a weighted plate on top of the fish to fully submerge all fillets.

4. Soak fish in brine 2 1/2 hours.

5. Place fish on racks and sprinkle with sesame seeds if desired.

6. Smoke to desired texture. Cooking time varies from 3-10 hours, depending on the smoker, volume of fish being smoked and outdoor conditions. Check frequently so as not to overcook.

7. Once fish has cooled, remove from racks, place in an airtight container and refrigerate overnight to enhance flavor.

Ingredients:

- 4 cups water
- 1 cup light corn syrup
- 1/2 cup Morton's Tender Quick
- 2 cups Saki
- 4 tablespoons white miso
- 2 teaspoons sesame oil
- 4 cloves garlic, minced
- 3" fresh ginger, peeled and thinly sliced
- 1/2 cup rice vinegar
- 1/4 cup lemon juice
- Sesame seeds, optional

Another addictive recipe from Bob and Peggy Cobb, this one yields a sweet-tasting fish with a candy-like coating.

Ingredients:

- 1/2 gallon water
- 1/2 cup non-iodized salt
- 1 tablespoon soy sauce
- 1 cup brown sugar
- 1 teaspoon fresh ground black pepper
- 1 tablespoon lemon pepper
- Dash of white wine
- Brown sugar

Instructions:

1. Mix the ingredients in a large bowl with a wire whisk until sugar is dissolved.
2. Soak fish, refrigerated, in brine 24 hours.
3. Rinse fish and place on racks.
4. Air dry 4 hours.
5. Sprinkle 1/8" brown sugar over fish.
6. Smoke 6-9 hours or to desired texture. Use 2-3 pans of chips.

A dark, rich-colored smoked fish that captures the smoke flavor of any chips used. The paprika adds a sweetness that is not overpowering.

Instructions:

1. Mix the ingredients in a large bowl with a wire whisk until sugar is dissolved.

2. Submerge fish in brine skin side down on the bottom layer, meat side down on the next layer. Repeat layering skin to skin, meat to meat.

3. Place a weighted plate on top of the fish to fully submerge all meat.

4. Soak fish in brine 2 hours.

5. Place on racks and sprinkle additional paprika and fresh black pepper over the moist fish.

5. Place on racks and air dry until pellicle is formed, 1-3 hours.

6. Smoke to desired texture. Cooking time varies from 3-10 hours, depending on the smoker, volume of fish being smoked and outdoor conditions. Check frequently so as not to overcook.

Ingredients:

- 1 1/2 quarts water
- 1/2 cup non-iodized salt
- 1/2 cup molasses
- 1/2 cup white sugar
- 1 teaspoon cayenne pepper (may add more for a hotter flavor)
- 2 teaspoons coriander
- 6 bay leaves
- 2 teaspoons paprika
- Freshly ground black pepper, to taste

Dill Infusion

An excellent, light, fresh-tasting recipe in which the fresh dill and lemon are greatly accentuated.

Ingredients:

- 6 cups water
- 1/2 cup Morton's Tender Quick
- 2 cups white sugar
- 1/2 cup lemon juice
- 1 ounce fresh baby dill

Instructions:

1. Mix the ingredients in a large bowl with a wire whisk until sugar is dissolved.

2. Submerge fish in brine skin side down on the bottom layer, meat side down on the next layer. Repeat layering skin to skin, meat to meat.

3. Place a weighted plate on top of the fish to fully submerge all fillets.

4. Soak fish in brine 2 1/2 hours. Do not oversoak as citric acids begin to "cook" the fish.

5. Smoke to desired texture. Cooking time varies from 3-10 hours, depending on the smoker, volume of fish being smoked and outdoor conditions. Check frequently so as not to overcook.

6. Fish may appear overcooked on the edges due to the citric acids. Remove from racks, place in an airtight container and refrigerate overnight. Fish will rehydrate.

Notes:

Substitute 2 tablespoons dry dill weed for fresh dill.

Dennis Richey is a man who is involved with sport fishing on many levels in an attempt to preserve it for future generations. This is his favorite recipe, one that puts out a slightly sweet, somewhat tangy, but not too salty end product.

Instructions:

1. Mix the ingredients.
2. Submerge fish in brine skin side down on the bottom layer, meat side down on the next layer. Repeat layering skin to skin, meat to meat.
3. Place a weighted plate on top of the fish to fully submerge all fillets.
4. Soak fish in brine 8-12 hours or overnight in the refrigerator.
5. Remove fish from brine and place in smoker.
6. Smoke to desired texture. Cooking time varies from 3-10 hours, depending on the smoker, volume of fish being smoked and outdoor conditions. Check frequently so as not to overcook.

Ingredients:

- 2 quarts water
- 2 cups brown sugar
- 1 cup rock salt
- 2 tablespoons granulated garlic
- 3 tablespoons Tabasco sauce

Notes:
Dill or other spices may be added to this recipe for desired flavor outcomes.

Hot Mustard with Honey Glaze

If you are a fan of the sharp hotness of mustard often served in Chinese restaurants, this recipe is a must-try. The bite of the mustard is tamed by the honey and both blend well with the wholesome smokey flavor.

Ingredients:

- 6 cups water
- 1 cup brown sugar
- 1/2 cup honey
- 1/3 cup non-iodized salt
- 1/3 cup soy sauce
- 2 tablespoons hot Chinese mustard
- 2 teaspoons liquid garlic or
  1 tablespoon minced garlic
- 1 teaspoon white pepper

GLAZE:

- 1 tablespoon hot Chinese mustard
- 1 tablespoon honey

Instructions:

1. Mix the brine ingredients in a large bowl with a wire whisk until sugar is dissolved.

2. Submerge fish in brine skin side down on the bottom layer, meat side down on the next layer. Repeat layering skin to skin, meat to meat.

3. Place a weighted plate on top of the fish to fully submerge all fillets.

4. Soak fish in brine 3 hours.

5. Place on racks.

6. Air dry until pellicle is formed, 1-3 hours.

7. Smoke to desired texture. Cooking time varies from 3-10 hours, depending on the smoker, volume of fish being smoked and outdoor conditions. Check frequently so as not to overcook.

8. Immediately after removing fish from the smoker, brush on honey glaze.

Notes:

The honey-mustard glaze also makes a great dipping sauce to serve alongside the fish.

Fellow angler, Jerry Bergman, is continually tinkering with smoking recipes. He likes this one most of all, and makes a great dip by mixing 1 cup smoked salmon, 1/2 cup mayonnaise, a squirt of sweet hot mustard and a dash of cayenne pepper.

Instructions:

1. Mix the ingredients in a large bowl.
2. Soak 24-48 hours in the refrigerator.
3. Rinse brine for a lighter flavor. Do not rinse for a more intense flavor.
4. Roll each piece of fish in sugar and place on racks.
5. About an hour before the fish is done, sprinkle with sugar.
5. Smoke until done.

Ingredients:

- 1 cup water
- 1/2 bottle Chardonnay
- 2 cups soy sauce
- 1 tablespoon pepper
- 1 tablespoon onion powder
- 1 tablespoon garlic powder
- 2 tablespoons Tabasco sauce
- 2-3 cups white or brown sugar
- 2 tablespoons of Lawry's seasoned salt
- Sugar

Notes:

Due to the extensive brine time, the final product is a firm meat with a very sweet flavor.

Walla Walla Plum

We have a golden plum tree that makes the best jam. Both sweet and tart, the flavors combine well with salmon and steelhead.

Ingredients:

- 1 1/2 quarts water
- 1 1/3 cups golden plum jam
- 1/2 cup hot water
- 1/2 cup white sugar
- 3/4 cup Morton's Tender Quick
- 2 Walla Walla onions, chopped

Instructions:

1. Mix the jam with 1/2 cup hot water and stir until liquified.
2. Mix the remaining ingredients and jam in a large bowl with a wire whisk until sugar is dissolved.
2. Submerge fish in brine skin side down on the bottom layer, meat side down on the next layer. Repeat layering skin to skin, meat to meat.
3. Place a weighted plate on top of the fish to fully submerge all fillets.
4. Soak fish in brine 3-4 hours.
5. Place on racks and air dry until pellicle is formed, 1-3 hours.
6. Smoke to desired texture. Cooking time varies from 3-10 hours, depending on the smoker, volume of fish being smoked and outdoor conditions. Check frequently so as not to overcook.

Notes:

Slightly sweet with a hint of onion. Many types of jam or marmalade can be substituted for the plum jam, just be sure not to use any low-sugar or sugar-free products.

Dry Brines

Bogue's Best

Noted Sacramento River guide, Mike Bogue, loves his fishing and his smoked fish. This is a recipe he's developed to accommodate his busy schedule.

Ingredients:

- 2 pounds Morton's Sugar Cure
- 1 pound brown sugar
- 2 teaspoons garlic salt
- 1 tablespoon seasoned salt
- Black pepper to taste

Instructions:

1. Mix the ingredients, except for pepper, in a large bowl.
2. Layer the fish in a large bowl, skin side down.
3. Cover with a layer of dry brine and continue layering fish and brine until done.
4. Soak in brine 8-12 hours. Lots of juice is produced, just let the fish soak in it.
5. Remove fish from brine and rinse well.
6. Blot fish dry and place on racks, add pepper.
7. Mix a bit of brown sugar with water to brush on the fish.
8. Put in smoker for 8-12 hours, brushing brown sugar mixture over fish every 2-3 hours.

Notes:

Nice firm texture, sweet with a hint of salt.

This recipe comes from good friend Russ Mathews, one of the hardest-working anglers on the river. As a result, he catches more fish than most people we know. This simple recipe is one he's refined over the years to make the process quick and easy.

Instructions:

1. Thoroughly mix salt and brown sugar.

2. Prior to placing the racks in the frame, sprinkle a liberal layer of the dry mixture over each piece of fish. Press the dry brine firmly into each piece of meat, and apply more mixture. Add approximately 1/4 inch of dry mixture, firmly packing it down. On thick pieces of fish, use a fork to work the dry brine into the meat.

3. Place the racks in the smoker frame, with drip pan removed, and let sit 8-12 hours. (The salt will draw moisture out of the fish, resulting in excessive dripping. Put the smoker racks in the kitchen sink during the brining process, allowing liquids to run down the drain.)

4. Before placing fish in the smoker, remove the sugar "crust" that forms on the fish. If you desire a very sweet finished product, the sugar can be left in place.

5. Sprinkle the fish with pepper, garlic salt or onion salt if desired.

6. Place the meat in the smoker and smoke to desired firmness.

Ingredients:

- 2 cups brown sugar
- 1/2 cup non-iodized salt
- Garlic salt, optional
- Onion salt, optional
- Black pepper, optional

Mediterranean Spiced

The distinct tastes of the spices traditionally used in many Greek, Spanish and Turkish dishes are accentuated by the smoking process.

Ingredients:

- 2 cups brown sugar
- 1/2 cup rock salt
- 2 tablespoons dried parsley
- 2 teaspoons garlic powder
- 2 teaspoons dried thyme
- 1 teaspoon anise seed, crushed
- 1 teaspoon cumin
- 1 teaspoon freshly ground black pepper
- Zest from 1 orange
- Honey for glaze, optional

Instructions:

1. Mix all ingredients, except honey.
2. Lay fish skin side down in a 9" x 11" glass casserole dish.
3. Sprinkle brine over fish.
4. Let sit for 2 hours.
5. Cover and place in refrigerator 12-15 hours.
6. Rinse fish, place on racks and let pellicle form, 1-3 hours.
7. Brush honey onto each piece, if an extra sweet flavor is desired.
8. Smoke to desired texture. Cooking time varies from 3-10 hours, depending on the smoker, volume of fish being smoked and outdoor conditions. Check frequently so as not to overcook.

Notes:

Mesquite and/or grape are the preferred chips in this recipe.

Kenai River guide and good friend, Brett Gesh, first shared the product of this recipe with us while working a sport show together. It came from his Aunt Zozie, and the moment we tasted it we knew it was a winner.

Instructions:

1. Mix the above ingredients in a small bowl.
2. Lay fillets out flat in glass pan, skin side down.
3. Sprinkle dry brine over fish, covering completely.
4. Let sit 12 to 24 hours. Drain liquid as it forms and discard.
5. Remove from brine and put on racks with larger pieces of fish on the bottom.
6. Sprinkle freshly ground pepper over fish if desired.
7. Smoke until done, use one pan of chips.

Ingredients:

- 1 cup white sugar
- 1 cup brown sugar
- 1/4 cup non-iodized salt
- Black pepper, optional

Notes:

Recipe lends itself well to experimentation. Add spices of choice, spice blends (Cajun) or hot pepper sauce to the brine if desired. Recommended wood chips: apple.

Doctor's One-Step

For decades, family friend Dr. Don Woomer has used this hassle-free, one-step cure he originally received from Dr. Dennis Conway. The end result is an excellent fish that readily picks up the smoke flavor of the chips.

Ingredients:

- Morton's Tenderquick Curing Salt
- Freshly ground black pepper

Instructions:

1. Place desired amount of Tenderquick on a large plate.
2. Roll each piece of fish in the Tenderquick, making sure to coat evenly on all sides.
3. Let fish sit in a large, flat pan 30 minutes. Take care that no piece of fish sits in the cure longer than 45 minutes.
4. Rinse fish under cold water. Fish feels slippery at first, gently rub the cure off so it is no longer slippery.
5. Lay each piece of fish skin side down on a clean bath towel or several paper towels.
6. Grind black pepper to desired taste over the fish.
7. Smoke to desired texture. Cooking time varies from 3-10 hours, depending on the smoker, volume of fish being smoked and outdoor conditions. Check frequently so as not to overcook.

Notes:

Any assortment of chips go well with this recipe.

Similar to wet brines using fresh herbs, this dry brine is easy and requires no fresh ingredients.

Instructions:

1. Mix the ingredients.
2. Lay fish skin side down in a 9" x 11" glass casserole dish.
3. Pour the brine over fish.
4. Let sit for 2 hours stirring occasionally.
5. Cover and place in refrigerator 12 hours.
6. Rinse fish, place on racks and let pellicle form, 1-3 hours.
7. Smoke to desired texture. Cooking time varies from 3-10 hours, depending on the smoker, volume of fish being smoked and outdoor conditions. Check frequently so as not to overcook.

Ingredients:

- 1 1/2 cups white sugar
- 1 cup brown sugar
- 1/2 cup rock salt
- 1/4 cup Italian seasoning
- 2 tablespoons dry dill weed
- 1 tablespoon dried parsley flakes
- 1 tablespoon granulated onion

High-Volume Dry Brine

Cliff Stiffler travels the West in search of salmon and steelhead, and catches an impressive number of fish during the course of a year. When we first tasted his smoked fish, we knew it was worth sharing.

Ingredients:

- 2 pounds dark brown sugar
- 1 heaping cup rock salt
- 1 teaspoon garlic powder
- 1 tablespoon black pepper

Instructions:

1. Mix ingredients by hand in a medium bowl.
2. Put a layer of fish in a large bowl, skin side down.
3. Cover the fillets with the dry brine.
4. Repeat layering fish with skin side down and a layer of dry brine.
5. Continue until all fish is used. Dump remaining dry brine on top.
6. Once moisture begins to seep out of the fish, work fillets around by hand every 30 minutes or so, for about 2 hours.
7. Make sure all pieces of fish are covered with brine, place plastic wrap over the bowl and refrigerate overnight.
8. Remove fish from brine and rinse in cold water, placing cleaned pieces on racks.
9. Let pellicle form if desired, not necessary.
10. Place in smoker 14-15 hours or until desired doneness. You may go through one bag of chips with this recipe. Be sure to rotate racks if smoking a lot of fish.
11. Remove from smoker, cool and place in the refrigerator for a day to mellow the flavor.
12. Eat or remove skin and vacuum seal for extended storage.

Notes:

Super flavor, hint of sweetness, light salt taste with a prevailing smoke flavor. This recipe can smoke up to 50 pounds of fish.

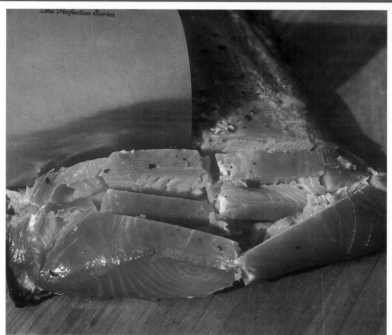

Scott and the two sons of Wayne and Judy Gammie grew up together, participating in sports, hunting and fishing from boyhood through high school. Scott will never forget the smell and taste of smoking fish at the Gammie house. Though Wayne, a retired butcher, has toyed with several labor-intensive brines, he always returns to his original.

Instructions:

1. Mix sugar and salt in a plastic or glass bowl.
2. Roll each piece of fish in the mixture, covering all sides.
3. Place in another plastic or glass bowl, skin side down on the bottom layer, meat side down on the next layer. Repeat layering skin to skin, meat to meat.
4. Place in the refrigerator for 18 hours, allowing the meat to sit in its own juices.
5. Remove fish from brine and rinse under cold water, placing cleaned pieces on racks.
6. Sprinkle black pepper on two racks, cajun seasoning (or other spice of choice) on the third rack to achieve two different tastes if desired.
7. Let pellicle form and place in the smoker.
8. Use two pans of hickory chips.
9. When done, remove skin and eat, or do as the Gammies and preserve for long-term storage by canning.

Ingredients:

- 3 cups brown sugar
- 1/2 cup non-iodized salt
- Black pepper (optional)
- Cajun seasoning (optional)

Notes:

The final product is firm and flakey, with a beautiful brown color on the outside. The taste is semisweet and delectable. Recommended wood chips: hickory.

Triple Pepper

Green, white and pink peppercorns can be found in many gourmet food stores. The subtle tastes of the three-pepper combination comes through in this savory smoking recipe.

Ingredients:

- 1 cup brown sugar
- 1 cup white sugar
- 1/2 cup rock salt
- 1 tablespoon cracked green peppercorns
- 1 tablespoon cracked white peppercorns
- 1 tablespoon cracked pink peppercorns

Instructions:

1. Crack whole peppercorns using a mortar and pestle or give them a few pulses in a food grinder.
2. Mix the above ingredients.
3. Lay fish skin side down in a 9" x 11" glass casserole dish.
4. Pour the brine over fish.
5. Let sit for 2 hours, stirring occasionally.
6. Cover and place in refrigerator 12-15 hours.
7. Rinse fish and place on racks.
8. For a sharper pepper flavor, grind your choice of pepper over the moist fish. To balance the pepper, sprinkle a bit of white sugar over the fish at the same time.
9. Air dry to allow pellicle to form, 1-3 hours.
10. Smoke to desired texture. Cooking time varies from 3-10 hours, depending on the smoker, volume of fish being smoked and outdoor conditions. Check frequently so as not to overcook.

Notes:
Peppery and sweet, a very traditional-tasting smoked fish.

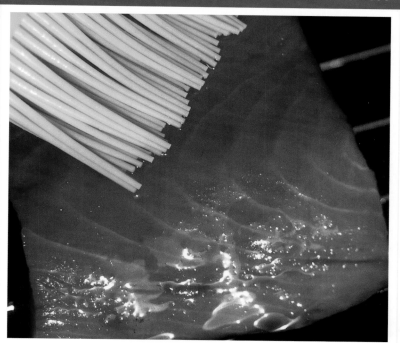

One of the most devoted and influential high school teachers we've ever known, John Connolly also loves spending time on the water. Initially given to John in the early 1980s by a friend who worked at a catering business, this recipe was one of the dishes they were famous for, and which John rates as his favorite.

Instructions:

1. Mix all ingredients in a glass bowl or crock.
2. Place the first layer of fish in the bowl, skin side down.
3. Spoon in a generous layer of mixture over the meat. Flesh down, place the next layer of meat atop the mixture. The third layer is laid skin to skin, covering the meat with a generous layer of mixture. Repeat layering, adding ingredients until done.
4. Weight fish down so it remains submerged in juices as they form.
5. Soak in the refrigerator 6 to 8 hours. If desiring a salty flavor, leave in the brine longer.
6. Remove fish from brine and rinse pieces under cold water.
7. Place on racks and let air dry for one hour, until pellicle forms.
8. Place in smoker using chips of choice and cook until done.
9. While still warm and on the racks, brush a coating of rum over each piece of fish. Though this may have no noticeable effect on the overall flavor, it will create a beautifully glossed finished product.

Ingredients:

- 4 cups rock salt
- 2 cups dark brown sugar
- 1 tablespoon white pepper
- 1 tablespoon garlic powder
- 1 tablespoon onion powder
- 3 tablespoons Morton's Tender Quick
- 1 cup rum
- 2-3 additional tablespoons of rum for brushing on later

Shake & Smoke

One of those "handful of this, handful of that" recipes, this can be tailored to meet any tastes, and used with as much or as little fish as available. Oregon angler and active Northwest Steelheader member, Mike Stortz, rates this as his preferred cure, and many of his friends agree.

Ingredients:

- Lawry's seasoned salt
- BBQ seasoning mix
- Lemon pepper
- Brown sugar

Instructions:

1. Skin fillet and cut into desired pieces for smoking.
2. Lay fish in a large, shallow pan.
3. Cover both sides of the fish lightly with Lawry's seasoned salt.
4. Sprinkle the desired amount of BBQ seasoning mix and lemon pepper.
5. Let fish sit in the dry seasonings for 2 1/2 to 3 hours. It will begin to juice up right away.
6. Poke the fish with a knife occasionally to help the seasonings marinate throughout the fillets.
7. After letting the fish sit in the salt mixture, lightly coat both sides of the fish with brown sugar. Poke the fish again with a knife to get the sugar deeper into the meat. Let the sugar soak into the fish for 1 hour.
8. Gently blot one side of the fish before putting it on the racks. Put the fish wet side down onto the racks so it will drip onto the fish on the lower rack. Place thicker pieces on the bottom racks.
9. Place in a preheated smoker. Watch fish closely as it will smoke faster than fish with the skin left on.
10. Use 2-4 pans of chips depending on the thickness of the fish. Check the fish for doneness each time you replace the chips.
11. Ready to serve immediately. Store fish in a ziploc bag in the refrigerator.

Notes:

Firm, sweet and peppery on the surface and very flavorful throughout. If using a thin cut of fish, go easy on the seasonings.

Full of flavor, this fish has less smokey taste and is dominated by spices. It lends itself well to dips and spreads.

Instructions:

1. Mix ingredients.
2. Lay fish skin side down in a 9" x 11" glass casserole dish.
3. Pour the brine over the fish.
4. Let sit for 2 hours, stirring occasionally.
5. Cover and place in refrigerator 12 hours.
6. Rinse fish, place on racks and let pellicle form, 1-3 hours.
7. Smoke to desired texture. Cooking time varies from 3-10 hours, depending on the smoker, volume of fish being smoked and outdoor conditions. Check frequently so as not to overcook.

Ingredients:

- 2 1/2 cups brown sugar
- 1/2 cup rock salt
- 1 tablespoon chili powder
- 1 tablespoon onion powder
- 1 tablespoon garlic powder
- 1 tablespoon white pepper
- 1/2 tablespoon cinnamon
- 2 teaspoons allspice
- 1 teaspoon cayenne pepper
- 1 teaspoon cloves
- 1 teaspoon nutmeg
- 1 teaspoon ginger

Basic Blend

Jay Jensen loves to fish, especially in winter when he's not working as an electrician. Those who have tasted this fish compare it to what's found in commercial smoke houses.

Ingredients:

- Non-iodized salt
- Brown sugar
- Honey

Instructions:

1. Using whole fillets with skin on, cover with thin layer of salt (2-3 tablespoons per fillet).

2. Drizzle on a light coating of honey (2-3 tablespoons per fillet), spread evenly by hand.

3. Cover with brown sugar and any additional spices desired.

4. Place in a glass casserole dish, stacking flesh to flesh, skin to skin.

5. Brine in the refrigerator 24 hours, making sure all fillets are in liquid.

6. Remove fish from brine and thoroughly rinse under cold water.

7. Cut to desired smoking-size fillets and place on smoker racks.

8. Apply a light coating of salt, honey and brown sugar for the glaze.

9. Air dry 8-12 hours.

10. Smoke with chips of choice to desired texture.

Notes:

Dill or jalapeño peppers go nicely in this recipe, add with the first application of brown sugar. Serve with honey mustard for added flavor.

Intensely flavorful on the surface, the fish carries a mild smoked flavor throughout.

Instructions:

1. Mix ingredients.

2. Lay fish skin side down in a 9" x 11" glass casserole dish.

3. Pour the brine over the fish.

4. Let sit for 2 hours, stirring occasionally.

5. Cover and place in refrigerator 12 hours.

6. Rinse fish, place on racks and let pellicle form, 1-3 hours.

7. Smoke to desired texture. Cooking time varies from 3-10 hours, depending on the smoker, volume of fish being smoked and outdoor conditions. Check frequently so as not to overcook.

Ingredients:

- 2 cups white sugar
- 1/2 cup rock salt
- 1/4 cup Cajun seasoning

As with brines, what wood a person chooses to smoke with comes down to personal preference. We know of people who detest any salmon or steelhead cooked over mesquite chips, while others rate these chips among their favorite. Then there are folks who can decipher only subtle differences in smokes.

At a family gathering we once served five selections of smoked salmon as an appetizer. Each was labeled according to the flavors they exhibited, but we didn't indicate if this was based on the brine or the wood chips. Nearly every person was convinced the fish were prepared with separate recipes, when in fact they were all soaked in the same brine, but were smoked with five different kinds of wood chips. This scenario shows how varying wood smoke can truly impact the overall taste of smoked fish.

The more you experiment with different woods, the more aware you'll grow of their unique flavorings. You can even take it a step further by mixing woods. One family friend prefers burning a 50/50 mix of cherry and alder chips, feeling they nicely complement one another.

For added flavor, chips can be soaked prior to burning. This phase can be taken beyond the level of simply soaking them in water to slow the burn rate, to soaking them in juices and/or alcohols to enhance the taste of the fish. Bourbon, brandy and wine are just a few alcohols known to embellish the flavor of smoked fish. Apple juice and grape juice are also popular for soaking chips. For even more variety, juniper berries, cinnamon sticks and other robust spices or herbs can also be soaked and burned with the chips.

Once in the pan, various spices can be added to the chips that will combust right along with them, again, adorning the flavor of the fish. Cumin, cloves, cinnamon sticks, cardamom, peppercorns and allspice are just some examples of what can be added to burning chips, impacting the flavor of the finished product.

Experimentation is the best way to discover appealing smoking recipes.

When it comes to selecting chips or chunks to burn, the choice may be dependent upon several factors: How hot your smoker gets, outside temperature, desired cook rates, and the texture of the desired end product. These all play a role in choosing a fuel type.

It's common knowledge that chips burn more readily than wood chunks. In fact, many people like placing sawdust in the bottom of their pans, covered by larger chips, so as to expedite the rate of burning.

Chips (left) and wood chunks (right) are the two most common forms of fuel for smoking fish.

But keep in mind that burning fuel releases more heat, and when combined with the heat output of the element within the smoker, can create a rather hot environment. This can be a desirable combination on cold days, when high heat is the objective, but on hot summer days, burning only one pan of chips may be necessary to keep the temperature lower inside the smoker. Soaking chips, so as to achieve a smoky, slow burn, is also common on hot, dry days. Once the chips or chunks begin to burn, vents can be closed to slow the cooking process. Conversely, on cold days, vents can be opened to increase the amount of heat.

Given the aforementioned options, we've come full circle, back to the kinds of wood chips available for use. What follows is a brief description of some of the woods commonly used in home smokers, and what type of flavor they exude. Keep in mind, these descriptions are based on personal experience, and again, may vary from one person to the next.

When soaked, wood chips burn slow, giving off a good deal of smoke.

- **ALDER:** One of the most common smoking woods in the Pacific Northwest, alder gives off a delicate smokey flavor while retaining a sweet quality. This is a widely preferred choice of woods when it comes to smoking salmon and steelhead.

- **HICKORY:** The widest-ranging wood used for smoking across North America, hickory is robust, known for its strong smoke flavor. Some say the heavy smoke flavor resembles the taste of bacon.

- **MESQUITE:** Another common smoking wood, mesquite exudes a strong woody taste. This is a good wood to combine with others when smoking.

- **MAPLE:** A strong smoke flavor is given off by this wood, while retaining a sweet taste.

- **OAK:** A popular smoking wood, oak produces a heavy smoke flavor that's great on thick salmon fillets.

- **MADRONE:** An excellent hot-smoking wood, the strong, pungent flavor given by this wood creates a unique flavor much like mesquite.

- **WILLOW:** Wild willow makes a delicate flavor that brings out the natural taste of mild steelhead meat.

- **BIRCH:** Results in a mildly smoked, somewhat sweet tasting fish.

- **ENGLISH WALNUT:** This heavy wood creates a strong smoke flavor that can be quite bitter when used alone. Walnut is good to combine with fruity woods.

- **MULBERRY:** This wood gives off a mild, sweet flavor, reminiscent of apple.

- **ASH:** A fast burning fuel, ash gives off a nice light flavor. These chips can be soaked to slow the burning process.

- **GRAPE:** Common throughout Europe, grape chips yield a tart taste combined with a sweet, aromatic flavor that fits somewhere between most hardwoods and other fruity woods.

- **OLIVE:** If you like the flavor of mesquite, but are in search of a less heavy taste, try olive wood.

- **ALMOND:** A sweet smoke flavor combined with a nutty taste makes this a great wood for smoking.

- **APPLE:** A fruity smoke flavor with a hint of sweetness, apple is one of the most common fruit woods to burn in smokers. Many people prefer this for the mild, yet somewhat complex flavor it creates.

- **CHERRY:** A widely used wood, cherry is one that can give off a range of flavors. A tart, fruity flavor is created by this wood, with some varieties pending on the edge of sweetness. It's a good wood to combine with others for a special flavoring.

- **PLUM:** If you like hickory, but desire a more mild and somewhat sweeter, fruity taste, try plum.

- **APRICOT:** A mild, sweet flavor results from the use of this wood.

- **LILAC:** A subtle, light tasting, almost flowery smoke flavor is created by lilac.

- **NECTARINE:** A mild, sweet flavor that falls somewhere between hickory and lighter fruitwoods can be expected when burning nectarine.

- **PEACH:** A somewhat wild, sweet flavor is created by this wood.

- **ORANGE:** If looking for a mid-range smokey flavor with a taste of mild fruitiness, orange wood is a good choice.

- **PEAR:** A sweet, somewhat wild flavor is the result of burning this wood.

■ PURCHASING WOOD CHIPS

Sawdust chips and larger wood chips or chunks are the two most common fuels for smoking fish. While can be acquired at many sporting goods stores, they can also be ordered direct from some companies.

When burning sawdust, be sure to find clean chips with a consistent burn rate and that are easy to work with. You can find these chips in most sporting goods stores or search the Internet.

The quality of the smoked fish you end up with is greatly influenced by how well the fish is cared for when caught. No matter which recipe you use, how long the fish may have soaked in a brine or what magic was pulled-off during the smoking process, the final outcome will only be as good as the care that went into the fish, and it begins the moment a fish is landed.

■ BLEEDING & CLEANING

As soon as a fish is landed, deliver a death blow to the head and immediately bleed the fish. Next, sever a gill so the fish will bleed out. Blood coagulates rapidly in dead fish, and becomes a hotbed for bacteria. The more blood that's present in a fish, the more potential for bacteria to thrive, thus fouling the taste. By bleeding a fish as soon as possible after being caught, the quality of meat dramatically increases.

If possible, it's even better to clean the fish, removing the entrails and gills. This assures that no stomach acids, digestive enzymes, tissue-destroying bacteria or excess blood will leach into the meat, otherwise denigrating its value. Anglers should note, some states do not allow fish entrails to be discarded into a stream, but this doesn't mean you can't clean your fish on the river. Simply take a bag or bucket to put the entrails into, disposing of the waste when you get home.

With ocean-caught fish, it's ideal to have the entrails fully removed within five minutes of being caught. This is because these voracious predators are aggressively feeding while at sea, and to accommodate the amount of prey they ingest, a heightened level of digestive enzymes are produced. Even when dead, these enzymes are at work inside the fish, digesting the membrane that separates the meat from the gut cavity and even the meat itself. By quickly removing the internal organs in any fish, the overall quality of the meat improves.

No matter where you are—in the ocean, on a river, in a boat or on the bank —it's best to get your fish on ice as quickly as possible. The sooner the meat can be cooled, the more firm and better tasting the flesh will be. During late fall and winter months, the air temperature is often cool enough to keep a fish until you've reached home. On hot summer days, it's best to have a cooler of ice handy. If bank fishing a river in the summer, it's not usually feasible to tote a bulky cooler filled with ice. In this case, clean the fish and hang it in a shady place. Find the coolest, darkest place to hang the fish, making sure direct sunlight does not strike the carcass during the course of the day.

Thoroughly cleaning a fish is the first step in attaining a tasty end product.

If fishing from a boat, be it at sea or on a river, having a cooler of ice is preferred, over tossing the fish into a metal box. Crushed ice is best, as it molds around the body of the fish, quickly cooling it. Ice cubes from the freezer also work, and can be stockpiled in a larger freezer days prior to hitting the water.

Once a fish is caught, break open a few bags of ice and surround the fish with it. To properly cool a fish, it's best if it can be gutted and the cavity packed with ice. Fish

The quicker fish can be put on ice, the better. Fillets, when placed on ice, cool much quicker than whole fish.

packed in ice within a good, airtight cooler can be kept for days. Be sure to open the bottom spigot to let the melted water drain, adding fresh ice as needed. Prior to placing the fish on ice or in the refrigerator, rinse thoroughly with cool tap water; this can remove up to 90% of the bacteria on the surface of the fish.

In our large coolers, we've kept multiple fillets up to five days, something that's handy if you want smoke fish fresh, or while gathering ingredients to create a special brine. When keeping fresh fish this long, add ice daily, making certain all fillets are surrounded by ice. Store-bought fish should be smoked within one to two days.

■ FREEZING BEFORE SMOKING

To produce the best-tasting, most nutritious fish, it's ideal to cook it fresh. But oftentimes this isn't possible, as large quantities of fish may be caught, or the ingredients needed for a particular recipe may not be on hand. For whatever reason, freezing raw fish is often inevitable. However, contrary to popular belief, you don't have to sacrifice meat flavor or value if it's properly frozen.

Fish is delicate, both in texture and flavor, and preventing air from reaching the frozen flesh, as well as water from escaping, is the objective. When exposed to air, meat loses moisture whereby the texture, color and even flavor quality is sacrificed. This is known as oxidation, which promotes freezer burn.

When freezing fish, there are certain steps that can be taken to maximize the quality of meat. Fish meat has no connective tissues, meaning as water freezes and expands in the flesh, it damages the meat. With fish, the more quickly the meat can be frozen, the better its eating quality will be. The best method is flash-freezing a fish at an extremely low temperature before storing it in a home freezer. But it's unrealistic for most of us to take our fish to a meat market or butcher shop for flash freezing, so what can we do to best preserve the meat in our home freezers?

When answering this question, all that must be kept in mind is that the quicker it can be frozen, the better tasting the meat will be. Quickly freezing fillets, or better yet, parts of fillets, is the goal. By cutting fillets into meal-size portions, the smaller-sized cuts freeze more rapidly. If you want to freeze a whole fish, it's best to freeze the fillets rather than the entire fish which takes too long to set up, resulting in mushy, pale meat once cooked.

Ideally, fish should be frozen after the process of rigor mortis is complete and the muscle of the fish is relaxed. If placing a fish on ice immediately after catching it, the rigor stage will be more subtle, and take longer to achieve. However, on hot days, failure to place a fish on ice immediately after catching will see it going through a harsh stage of rigor, which may cause flesh damage. Once caught, it's best to keep the fish as cool as possible, and to freeze it once it's been filleted.

The flavor of your fish is dependent on how you have handled it from the time it's caught to the time it goes into the freezer. The meat quality will only be as good as it was when you froze it. If a fish is improperly handled and cared for prior to freezing, oxidation of fats can begin; not even freezing can stop this chemical change. This will create a very undesirable flavor and color change. To help prevent this, carry the fish by the head, not the tail, and take measures to remove all blood prior to freezing. When butchering, routinely wash the knife and handle the meat with utmost care, keeping it on a clean surface at all times.

To attain optimum value, fish should be smoked within the first three months of being placed in the freezer, not for safety reasons, but because the quality of meat declines after this time period. Then again, there are ways to extend its shelf life in the freezer.

When storing meat in the freezer, vacuum sealing is regarded as the best way to go. We've kept fish this way for up to a year in the freezer. This technique removes as much air from the package as possible, which is the most important step when freezing fish. When thawing these packages, it's vital to remove the meat as soon as it's thawed, as mold quickly forms in this medium, even when thawed in the refrigerator. Note, vacuum sealing does not preserve fish, it only removes the air from around it. It's vital to place sealed packages in the freezer as quickly as possible.

If a food sealer is not accessible, an alternative is placing the meat in sealable baggies, forcing the air out by placing it in water. With only a tiny portion of the baggy left open, submerge the baggy in a sink full of cold water, bottom end first. As the water pushes against the fish, it forces air out the top of the bag. Once to the top, close the bag when the air has been removed, making certain no water enters the bag. Wrapping this in a layer of freezer paper will allow the meat to be kept frozen for extended periods.

If you know the frozen fish will be smoked within a few months of storing, wrap the fillet in two layers of freezer paper, or other containers designed for freezing. Canning jars, plastic containers and plastic wrap made especially for the freezer are all good options. While the specialized freezer plastic wrap is more costly than the standard wrap, it's best for preserving fish. First wrapping the fish in plastic wrap, then in a layer of freezer paper is good for keeping air out, further protecting against freezer burn. You can also double wrap small fillets in the plastic wrap, then place in freezer-grade sealable bags for added protection.

For long-term freezer storage, vacuum sealing fillets is ideal.

Prior to placing fish in the freezer, be sure to properly label each package. Include the date caught, species and where it was caught. We even like indicating the condition of the fish.

Keep in mind home freezers are not designed for rapid freezing. Avoid stacking fish on top of one another, as the resulting slow set-up time fosters bacterial growth and enzymatic spoilage. The faster your fish freezes, the less cell destruction you will have, the better the overall meat quality will be. Once frozen solid, we like stacking our fish for easy identification and to keep close track of what's in the freezer.

It's best to work fast when placing fillets inside the freezer. The longer one stands with the door open, the more cool air is being removed from the unit, the longer it will take for the fillets to freeze. Some units have areas that freeze faster than others, usually in direct contact with the freezing coils, floor or walls. This is where you'll want to place your fish. Avoid placing fish inside the door of the freezer, as this takes the longest to freeze and is not an optimal spot for long-term storage.

When preparing to smoke fish that has been frozen, thaw them as slowly as possible. A slow thawing process is crucial, as it reduces drip loss, where excess moisture exits the fish, decreasing its nutritional value and creating an undesirable texture. Slowly thawing a fish also protects against the growth of surface bacteria. Once a fish has been thawed, it should never be refrozen.

Be sure the fillet is fully thawed before cutting it into smaller sizes for brining, so as to prevent damaging flesh. Cutting and preparing partially frozen fillets can degrade the overall meat value, as the outside edges are softer than the center, thus damaging the meat. However, fresh fish can be cut to desired-size smoking fillets, then placed in the freezer, making for easy handling when it comes time for smoking.

■ DEBONING FILLETS

A salmon or steelhead fillet is not truly boneless. Look or feel closely and you'll notice the ends of the lateral bones protruding from the length of the fish, just above the midsection. In an unsmoked fish, these bones cannot be removed without damaging the meat. The bones actually turn up toward the spine, and trying to extract them from a fillet separates the thickest, most desirable cut of meat.

If you're intent on removing the bones prior to eating, do so once the meat has been smoked. At this time, the tips of bone project from the meat and can be easily be removed with your fingers or tweezers.

The best time to debone a fish is once the meat has been smoked.

Canning smoked fish is one of the best ways to ensure long-term preservation. But for younger generations who may not have been raised in households where canning was a part of the lifestyle, conquering this technique can be difficult, even intimidating. That's why we called upon Master Food Preserver Sharon Weber for assistance on this topic. Sharon is a volunteer with the Oregon State University Lane County Extension service, specializing in food preservation.

When preserving any food, safety is the number-one concern. Your local extension office can be a wealth of information and most have volunteers that can help you access their resources for any questions you may have that are not answered here. They may also have free classes you can take to learn, hands-on.

Prior to smoking and canning any salmon or steelhead, be certain the fish is of good quality. Make sure all blood is removed, the fish has been scaled and any bruised flesh has been removed. The process of smoking and canning will not improve the quality of your fish.

Even when smoked fish is placed in the refrigerator, within two to three weeks, the meat can grow bacteria that cause botulism. Because smoked fish has a short shelf life, it must be either frozen or canned for long-term preservation. Due to the dramatic loss of meat quality once frozen, it's not advisable to freeze any smoked fish unless prepared in a food sealer. The absolute best way to preserve your smoked fish is through canning. When canning salmon and steelhead, you must use a pressure canner in order to destroy the Clostridium botulinum spores.

Be aware that canning smoked fish tends to darken the overall color, dry the meat and increase the smoked flavor. As the smoke taste can be overpowering, if you know you're going to be canning the smoked fish ahead of time, you may want to go light on the smoke. This means smoking the fish for about two hours, in temperatures ranging between 140 to 160°F. Some folks prefer a dry, strong smoke flavor, so smoke their fish as normal when canning. It should also be noted that it's typical for fluids drawn from the fish to collect in the bottom of the jar.

Canning smoked fish is initially time-consuming, but rewards your efforts all year long.

Keep in mind, lightly smoking fish means it will not be done when removed from the smoker. Because of this fact, DO NOT eat lightly smoked salmon, as it is unsafe. When you correctly process it in a pressure canner, any bacteria present will be killed. Thus, it's important to only smoke the amount of fish you are going to be able to can in the same day. It's vital to clean and fully sanitize your work area after having worked with lightly smoked salmon or steelhead.

When canning these fish, you must use a 16-or 22-quart pressure canner, as there are no tested processing times for smaller pressure canners or quart jars. It is never safe to reduce the processing times or pressure when you are canning. If using a dial-gauge canner, make certain to check it once a year for accuracy and to see that the gasket is in good working condition.

With those points in mind, here are the simple, yet important steps to closely follow when canning smoked salmon and steelhead:

1. Once the fish has been smoked, keep the skin on and pack loosely or tightly into pint or half-pint jars. How much fish you place in a jar is left to personal preference. Some people always can their fish in pint jars, as the end product in half-pint jars may be unacceptable for the jars may float when being processed. There is no need to add liquid to the jar, and be sure to leave 1" of headspace in the jar.

2. Wipe jar rims clean with a paper towel that has been moistened with vinegar. This will help achieve a good seal any time you are canning fatty fish. Place lid on and screw the ring on snugly. Process half-pint and pint jars for 110 minutes. The pressure is dependent upon your elevation and whether you're using a weighted-gauge canner or a dial-gauge.

DIAL-GAUGE CANNER

- Sea level to 2,000' elevation, use 11 pounds pressure.
- 2,001 to 4,000' elevation, use 12 pounds pressure.
- 4,001 to 6,000' elevation, use 13 pounds pressure.
- 6,001 to 8,000' elevation, use 14 pounds pressure.

WEIGHTED-GAUGE CANNER

- Sea level to 1,000' elevation, use a 10-pound weight.
- Over 1,000' in elevation, use a 15-pound weight.

3. After it has been processed for the appropriate amount of time, remove the canner from the heat. Let the pressure return to zero before opening the canner. **DO NOT** try to get the pressure to drop more quickly than it does on its own. All processing times figure-in getting up to temperature and cool-down time.

4. Remove the jars from the canner and let cool.

5. Test all jars in 24 hours to make sure they got a good seal. If there are only one or two that didn't seal, you can put those in the refrigerator and consume them right away, or place them in the freezer. If freezing, remove screw band to prevent jar from breaking, it can be reattached once the meat is frozen. If three or more jars did not seal, remove the old lids and rings from every jar, put on new lids and tighten the screw rings down. Reprocess all jars in the canner for the entire length of time.

6. Label, date and store the jars in a cool, dark, clean and dry place. Avoid storing them in direct sunlight, near a furnace, by hot pipes or in a setting where they may freeze, as this could impact the quality of the fish and even lead to spoilage.

Before opening any home canned salmon or steelhead, it's best to check for spoilage. If the lid is bulging before removal, if liquid spurts out, it smells foul or if there is any mold, it is **NOT** safe to eat. Do not taste anything that is questionable. Also, keep in mind that botulism is odorless, colorless and tasteless. You must depend on safe and proper canning methods when working with fatty fish.

Once a jar of canned fish has been opened, it's wise to wash off the lid, even if you are going to throw it away. If you're going to reuse the lid on the opened jar, it's imperative to clean the lid before reattaching.

As an added safety measure, it's best to heat home canned fish (and any seafood) prior consumption. To destroy any toxins that may have formed, boil the fish for 10 minutes on the stovetop. You may also achieve this by heating it in the oven, in the jar you canned it in. To do this, remove the lid and place a meat thermometer into the jar, with the tip in the center of the jar. Cover the jar with foil and place in a preheated oven at 350°F. It will take approximately 30-35 minutes for the thermometer to register 185°F, the steelpeature at which the fish is done.

Canning is the best way to store smoked fish for any length of time. It also makes for tasty treats in the field.

Favorite Recipes

Some of our favorite family dishes include smoked fish. Depending on the smoking brine you use, these recipes can turn out different every time. Many of the recipes accentuate the flavor of the smoked fish be it Dill Infused smoked salmon with Salmon Dill Potato Salad or Herb Medley smoked salmon with Colorful Spiral Salad. Experiment around and be sure to make note of your favorite flavor combinations.

Angel Hair Pasta with Salmon & Spinach

Ingredients:

- 1/2 cup smoked salmon or steelhead
- 1/4 cup butter
- 2/3 cup whipping cream
- 1/3 cup milk
- 1/2 cup parmesan cheese
- 1/2 cup spinach, cut into strips
- Pepper to taste
- 8 ounces angel hair pasta

Instructions:

Work fish into bite-sized flakes, certain all bones are removed, set aside. Melt butter in a heavy skillet, add cream and milk, stirring constantly until thickened. Add smoked salmon, parmesan cheese, pepper and spinach. Simmer on low heat 5-10 minutes. Cook pasta to desired tenderness. Toss together and serve immediately.

Salmon Dill Potato Salad

Ingredients:

- 1 cup flaked, smoked salmon
- 4 cups cooked potatoes, peeled and cubed
- 2 cups celery, chopped
- 1/2 cup dill pickles, minced
- 3 tablespoons scallions, thinly sliced
- 2 cups mayonnaise

- 2 tablespoons mustard
- 1 tablespoon fresh dill or 1 teaspoon dry dill
- 1 teaspoon garlic salt
- 1 teaspoon granulated onion
- 1 teaspoon lemon pepper

Instructions:

Boil unpeeled potatoes until tender and easily pierced with a fork. Cool, peel and cube potatoes. Work fish into bite size flakes, certain all bones are removed. In a large mixing bowl, combine potatoes, celery, pickles and scallions. In a small mixing bowl combine mayonnaise, mustard and seasonings. Add mayonnaise mixture to potato mixture and gently combine. Last, add smoked salmon and gently mix in. Garnish with scallions or chives. Keep refrigerated.

Mushroom & Rice Bake

Ingredients:

- 1 1/2 cups smoked salmon or steelhead
- 4 tablespoons butter
- 1 green pepper, diced
- 1 pound mushrooms, diced
- 1 zucchini squash, diced

- 1 can cream of mushroom soup
- 1/2 cup milk
- 3 cups cooked rice
- 1 cup French fried onions, divided
- Black pepper to taste

Instructions:

Separate fish into bite-sized pieces, certain all bones are removed, set aside. Melt butter in a medium skillet. Add peppers and sauté 2-4 minutes. Add mushrooms and squash and sauté an additional 2-3 minutes. In a large mixing bowl whisk together the soup and the milk. Add all remaining ingredients and 1/2 cup of the French fried onions, stir just to combine. Take special care not to break up the fish. Pour into a buttered, 9" by 11" casserole pan. Bake, uncovered, in a preheated oven at 350° for 30-35 minutes or until heated throughout. Sprinkle the remaining French fried onions on the casserole during the last 10 minutes of cooking time.

Ingredients:

- 1 1/2 cups smoked salmon or steelhead
- 1 cup mayonnaise
- 1 cup parmesan cheese
- 1 6-ounce can black olives, sliced
- 1 4-ounce can fire-roasted mild green chilies, diced
- 1 cup Monterey Jack cheese
- 1/2 cup cheddar cheese

Instructions:

Work fish into small flakes, certain all bones are removed, set aside. Mix remaining ingredients, reserving 1/2 cup parmesan cheese for the top of dip. Gently fold smoked salmon into the mayonnaise and cheese mixture. Spread into a glass pie pan or divide among 2-3 ovenproof dishes. Top with remaining parmesan cheese. Bake in a preheated oven at 400° for 25 minutes. Cool a few minutes before serving. Serve with plain tortilla chips. This recipe doubles easily for a crowd, use a 9"x 13" casserole dish.

Salmon Puffs

Ingredients:

FILLING:

- 1 1/2 cups smoked salmon
- 1 8-ounce package whipped cream cheese (at room temperature)
- 2 tablespoons finely sliced green onion

PUFFS:

- 1 cup 7-Up
- 1/2 cup butter or margarine
- 1 cup flour
- 4 large eggs

Instructions:

Bring 7-Up and butter to a boil in a medium saucepan. Add flour. Remove from heat. Add eggs one at a time and beat with a wooden spoon after each. Drop mixture, by teaspoonful, on a cookie sheet. Bake in a preheated oven at 350° for about 10 minutes (watch closely). They should be lightly browned on top. Let puffs cool. Work fish into tiny flakes, be certain all bones are removed. Blend fish, salt, pepper, cream cheese and green onion together. Slice puffs in half and stuff with filling. Makes 25-30 puffs. Serve immediately or keep refrigerated. These puffs also make a delicious dessert filled with vanilla pudding.

Ingredients:

- 1 cup smoked salmon or steelhead
- 3 tablespoons sundried tomato pesto (recipe follows or use prepared)
- 1/4 cup fresh basil leaves
- 1/4 cup roasted red and/or yellow sweet peppers, chopped

- 1 cup smoked gouda cheese, cubed
- 2 cups uncooked vegetable spiral pasta
- Freshly grated parmesan cheese, if desired

Instructions:

Cook pasta as directed on package. Cool and set aside. Gently stir pesto into pasta. Work fish into bite sized flakes, certain all small bones are removed. Add basil, fish, peppers and cheese, toss lightly. Serve at room temperature, but refrigerate any unused portion. Top with freshly grated parmesan cheese. A tasty variation to this recipe is substituting basil pesto for the sundried tomato pesto.

SUNDRIED TOMATO PESTO:

- 1/4 cup sundried tomatoes packed in olive oil
- 1/4 cup toasted pine nuts
- 1/3 cup parmesan cheese

- 2 small cloves garlic
- Mix in a food processor until well blended.

Pepper Jack Quesadillas with Cilantro Salsa

Ingredients:

- 2 cups smoked salmon or steelhead
- 12 large flour tortillas
- 2 cups pepper jack cheese
- 2 cups mild cheddar cheese

SALSA:

- 2 large red tomatoes, chopped
- 1 yellow or green bell pepper, seeded and chopped
- 1/3 cup onion, chopped
- 1 cup cilantro leaves
- 2 cloves garlic, minced
- Juice of 1 lime
- 1/2 teaspoon cumin
- Salt to taste
- Sour cream for garnish, if desired

Instructions:

Combine all ingredients for salsa and let sit while preparing quesadillas. Work fish into bite-sized flakes, make certain all small bones are removed. Grate and mix the two cheeses. Place one tortilla in a hot skillet or griddle. Cover with 1/2 to 3/4 cup cheese blend. Sprinkle about 1/3 cup smoked fish evenly over the cheese. Top with another tortilla. Once the tortilla is lightly browned on the bottom, turn over and brown the other side. Remove from pan and use a pizza cutter to slice the quesadilla on a cutting board. Serve pie-shaped wedges with fresh salsa.

Ingredients:

- 1 cup smoked salmon or steelhead
- 8 ounces cream cheese, softened and divided
- 2 tablespoons mayonnaise
- 1/3 cup pesto (recipe follows or use prepared)
- 4 large tortillas, wraps or flatbread of choice

Instructions:

Work fish into tiny flakes, make certain all small bones are removed. In a small bowl, mix fish with 4 ounces of the cream cheese and 2 tablespoons mayonnaise. Lay the tortilla, wrap or flatbread on a cutting surface. On 1/3 of the wrap, spread the salmon mixture, on another 1/3 spread the pesto and on the last 1/3 spread the plain cream cheese. Be sure to cover the entire surface of the tortilla, wrap or flatbread. Starting on the salmon side, tightly roll the wrap, sealing on the cream cheese side. Cut into 1" rounds, secure with a toothpick and serve.

PESTO:

- 1 cup loosely packed, washed basil leaves
- 2 small cloves garlic
- 2 tablespoons toasted pine nuts
- 1/3 cup grated parmesan cheese
- 2 tablespoons olive oil
- Salt and pepper to taste

Mix in a food processor until well blended.

Individual Tarts

Ingredients:

- 2/3 cup smoked salmon or steelhead
- 2 eggs
- 1/4 cup milk
- 1/3 cup Swiss cheese, grated
- 2 tablespoons green onion, chopped

- 1 tablespoon fresh parsley, chopped
- Dash of black pepper
- Dash of cayenne pepper
- 1 11-inch-diameter pie crust, rolled flat
- Cherry tomatoes, for garnish

Instructions:

Using a round 2 1/2"-diameter cookie cutter or jar lid, cut circles from pie crust. Press into greased mini-muffin pans. Prick bottom of tart shell with a fork. Bake in a preheated oven at 400° 5-7 minutes. Cool completely before adding filling. Work fish into tiny flakes, making certain all small bones are removed. In a medium bowl, whip eggs with a wire whisk until frothy. Add remaining ingredients, except for cherry tomatoes, and mix thoroughly. Fill cups 3/4 full of egg mixture. Bake at 325° for 12-15 minutes or until set and golden brown. Top with a wedge of cherry tomato. Makes 12 tarts.

Sensational Dip

Ingredients:

- 1 cup smoked salmon or steelhead
- 8 ounces cream cheese, at room temperature
- 1/2 cup sour cream
- 1/4 cup chives, finely chopped
- 1 teaspoon Worcestershire sauce
- 1/2 teaspoon garlic powder
- 1/2 teaspoon lemon pepper

Instructions:

Work fish into small flakes, certain all bones are removed, set aside. In a medium bowl, mix the remaining ingredients until smooth. Gently fold fish into dip mixture. The dip can be served right away, or cooled in the refrigerator for two hours, shaped into a ball and rolled in crushed almonds or walnuts for a decorative presentation. To use as a sandwich spread add 2-4 tablespoons mayonnaise to the mix. Refrigerate unused portions for future use.

Sushi Rolls

Ingredients:

- 4 cups cooked medium-grain white rice
- 1/2 cup rice vinegar
- 4 tablespoons sugar
- 2 teaspoons salt
- 1 package nori (roasted seaweed)
- 2 cups smoked salmon
- 3 carrots, cut in long, narrow strips
- 1 red pepper, cut in long, narrow strips
- 1 cucumber, cut in long, narrow strips
- 1/2 cup fresh cilantro leaves
- Sesame seeds
- Wasabi paste
- Soy sauce
- Rice vinegar
- Bamboo mat

Instructions:

Prepare all ingredients. Steam carrots and red pepper in rice vinegar if desired. Work fish into large bite-sized pieces, be certain all bones are removed and set aside. Mix vinegar, sugar and salt and set aside.

The next step is best with two people. As soon as rice is cooked, transfer into a casserole dish. Pour vinegar mixture over rice and immediately begin to gently stir together. While one person is stirring the rice mixture, another person needs to be fanning the rice. Mix until there is no remaining liquid, no more than 2 minutes. Cover rice with damp towel.

Lay a nori wrapper on bamboo mat. Slightly wet hands and scoop approximately 2/3 cup of rice, spreading in a thin layer. Add vegetables, smoked salmon, cilantro and sprinkle sesame seeds. Gently but firmly roll nori, squeezing down on the bamboo mat to shape as desired. Unroll the mat and place the roll on a cutting surface. Using a very sharp, damp knife, cut into portions 1/2" to 1" thick. Serve with wasabi and soy sauce.

Cheesy Quiche

Ingredients:

- 1 10-inch uncooked pie crust
- 2 cups smoked salmon
  or steelhead
- 6 eggs
- 2/3 cup milk
- 1/2 teaspoon onion powder

- 1/4 teaspoon black pepper
- 1/4 teaspoon paprika
- 2 tablespoons fresh, chopped parsley
- 1 tomato, diced
- 1/2 cup grated cheddar cheese
- 1/2 cup grated jack cheese

Instructions:

Separate fish into bite-sized pieces, certain all small bones are removed, set aside. Beat eggs, milk, salt, pepper and paprika together, set aside. Place the uncooked pie crust into a pie pan. Sprinkle flaked fish, tomato and parsley evenly in the pie shell. Sprinkle cheddar and jack cheeses over the fish. Pour the egg mixture over everything in the pie pan. Bake in a preheated oven at 350° for 35-45 minutes or until set and golden brown.

When it comes to smoking salmon and steelhead, there are many questions that arise. These are ones that often keep people from smoking more fish, or worse yet, from experimenting with a variety of recipes. The multitude of smoked fish flavors that can be attained provide a gratifying taste alternative when compared to what most people are used to. But, if we try straying from what we know, and turn out a poor batch of smoked fish, the chances of future experimentation declines.

This trouble-shooting section is meant to answer basic questions that we've experienced through personal trial and error, and what's been brought to our attention by fellow, avid smokers. The purpose is to offer a quick and simple remedy, something that will enhance the creation of each and every batch of fish you smoke.

- **PROBLEM:** No pellicle is forming.
- **REMEDY:** If any form of citrus or alcohol is used in the brine, it can keep a pellicle from forming. If no citrus is used, make sure there is proper air movement around the fish, that all sides of the fish are exposed and that it is not in direct sunlight. An oscillating fan may need to be placed on the fish if air movement is lacking or if conditions are too humid. Also, check to see if the meat itself exhibits freezer burn as this can prolong the formation of a pellicle.

- **PROBLEM:** Final product is not done, or larger pieces taking too long.
- **REMEDY:** Wrap smoker in heat blanket on cold days. Can also finish the fish in the oven, on low heat (200°-250°).

- **PROBLEM:** Some pieces not done, others too done.
- **REMEDY:** Prior to placing in smoker, situate the largest fillets on the bottom rack, closest to the element. The smaller pieces go on top, farthest from the element. Periodically check for doneness. When the smaller, top pieces are done, remove, leaving the larger pieces in the smoker to continue smoking.

Cleaning smoker racks prior to each smoking session ensures a better tasting fish.

- **PROBLEM:** Fat oozing from smoked fish, or the flesh overcooked on the outside.
- **REMEDY:** The smoker got too hot, too quickly. On temperature-controlled smokers, lower the starting temperature and close all ducts. On fixed-element units, don't start the smoker until the fish is placed inside the unit. You can also slightly offset the lid, to allow heat to escape out the top. If using large wood chips, try soaking them first, as this will slow their burn rate, decreasing the amount of direct heat.

On cold days, an insulating blanket is the safest, most effective way to keep in heat and smoke.

- **PROBLEM:** Fish not getting done in cold outside temperatures.
- **REMEDY:** Wrap your smoker in a specially designed heat blanket. If safety is a concern, do not insulate your smoker, but remove the fish and finish cooking on low heat in the oven.

- **PROBLEM:** A strong, burnt taste is evident on the fish.
- **REMEDY:** With a stiff wire brush, be sure to clean the racks and even the inside walls of your smoker after each use. This will remove the soot buildup which, when reheated, can influence the flavor of your fish. You can also wash the racks in the dishwasher, keeping them clean.

Keeping fresh foil on the drip pan guards against burnt flavors.

- **PROBLEM:** The drip pan is corroding.
- **REMEDY:** As fats and oils drip from fish in the smoker, they fall on to the drip pan, where they continue to cook, often times only inches away from the heat source. The result is a strong burnt smell then can not only taint the taste of your fish, but greatly shorten the life of the drip pan. Prior to each smoking session, wrap the drip pan in aluminum foil, which will catch the drippings and can be disposed of when finished smoking.

If short on time, rinse and store brined fillets in the refrigerator, rather than keep them in the brine, where they may acquire an overpowering taste.

- **PROBLEM:** The fish soaked in the brine too long.
- **REMEDY:** When removing fish from the brine, thoroughly rinse under cold tap water to avoid an overpowering flavor. If the brine has a high salt ratio, sugar or other spices can be sprinkled on the meat once on the rack, to tame the salty flavor.

- **PROBLEM:** Not enough time to remove fish from brine, let pellicle form, and place in smoker.
- **REMEDY:** Rather than leaving fish in the brine overnight, remove from the brine, rinse under cold tap water (if directed in the recipe) and place in a covered bowl in the refrigerator. The next day, remove and place on racks to air dry. Though it takes longer for the pellicle to form in this way, often resulting in a subtle glaze, it does work in a pinch.

On cold days, or where the fish is not getting done quickly enough in the smoker, finish off on low heat in the oven.

- **PROBLEM:** Some pieces of fish not done on all sides.
- **REMEDY:** Do not let the fillets come in contact with one another in the smoker, as this will prevent smoke and heat from reaching those spots.

- **PROBLEM:** Final product is too dry.
- **REMEDY:** If any form of citrus is used, it may actually start cooking the fish in the brine. When this fish is exposed to heat within the smoker, the "cooked" flesh turns dry. With any dry fish, be it from citrus or simple oversmoking, remove from racks and cool slightly. Place in a glass bowl, cover with plastic wrap and store in the refrigerator overnight. This will rehydrate most if not all of the dried meat, revitalizing its overall quality that may have appeared lost.

- **PROBLEM:** Final product is too dry.
- **REMEDY:** If your smoker allows, place a pan of water in with the fish. This will help keep the fish moist, especially when cooked on hot summer days.

During fly and bee season, protect air-drying fish with cheesecloth.

- **PROBLEM:** Meat overcooking in hot weather.
- **REMEDY:** Cut smoking time down when it is hot and dry outside and check fish often. You can also cut thicker fillets, which take more time to cook. Finally, try burning a smaller portion of wood chips, as this will reduce heat production.

- **PROBLEM:** Too much fat is quickly bubbling to surface of meat.
- **REMEDY:** Start smoking at a lower heat on temperature-controlled units, or with the lid open on fixed units. More heat can be added later in the smoking process, once the fats have set up.

- **PROBLEM:** Going through too many wood chips.
- **REMEDY:** Soak them in water or another desired liquid to slow the burning process.

- **PROBLEM:** Flies and bees are attracted to fish while air drying.
- **REMEDY:** Cover with cheesecloth or take in the house, placing an oscillating fan on the fish to form pellicle.

- **PROBLEM:** Finished product too salty even when cutting back on salt ratios.
- **REMEDY:** Decrease time in the brine, or switch to rock salt as it has a slower dissolving rate than smaller-grained salts.

- **PROBLEM:** Finished product has strong taste of smoke and/or brine only on surface, not throughout the meat.
- **REMEDY:** Place fish in baggies or covered plastic bowl and put in refrigerator for 24 hours to absorb the flavors.

When searching for a smoker, find one that fits your needs and volume of fish you anticipate handling. Luhr-Jensen's Big Chief will accommodate 50 pounds of fillets.

To learn which flavors can be created, test not only brines, but a selection of woods as well.

Recipe Index
Wet Brines

Dry Brines

Favorite Recipes

Index

Recipe Notes

Scott & Tiffany Haugen were born and raised in Oregon's Willamette Valley, near the breathtaking McKenzie River. Growing up, both families depended on wild game as a staple, and salmon and steelhead played an important role.

After marriage, Scott & Tiffany spent several years living in the Alaskan Arctic, where they adopted a subsistence lifestyle. Traveling the globe, the couple later called Sumatra, Indonesia home. Together the Haugens have traveled to nearly 30 countries. Today the Haugens live near where they both grew up, raising two sons, Braxton and Kazden.

PLANK COOKING
The Essence of Natural Wood

By Scott & Tiffany Haugen

In Plank Cooking: The Essence of Natural Wood, globe-trotting authors, Scott & Tiffany Haugen, share some of the world's most exquisite flavors. Thai red curry prawns, Achiote pork roast, pesto couscous stuffed chicken, and caramelized bananas are just a few of the unique recipes brought to life in this fully illustrated, one-of-a-kind book.

In the oven or on a grill, plank cooking is fun and simple. This book outlines how to master the art of plank cooking, from seasoning planks to detailed cooking tips in over 100 easy-to-follow recipes. Though exotic tastes prevail, the ingredients used in Plank Cooking are easy to find in most grocery stores. Full color; 6 x 9; 152 pages

Spiral SB: $19.95   **ISBN: 1-57188-332-0**

COOKING SALMON & STEELHEAD
Exotic Recipes From Around the World

By Scott & Tiffany Haugen

This is not your grandmother's salmon cookbook. The long-time favorites are included and also unique yet easy-to-prepare dishes, like Cabo fish tacos and Tuscan pesto. This cookbook includes: Appetizers, soups & salads, entrees, one-dish meals, exotic tastes, marinades & rubs, outdoor cooking, pastas, stuffed fish, plank cooking, wine selection, scaling and fileting your catch, choosing market fish, cooking tips, and so much more. The Haugens have traveled to and studied cuisines in countries

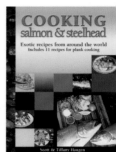

around the world—including the Caribbean, Asia, and Europe—your kitchen is not complete without a copy of **Cooking Salmon & Steelhead.**

Spiral SB: $24.95   **ISBN: 1-57188-291-X**

SUMMER STEELHEAD
FISHING TECHNIQUES

By Scott Haugen

Scott Haugen is quickly becoming known for his fact-filled, full-color fishing books. This time Haugen explores summer steelhead, including: understanding summer steelhead; reading water; bank, drift, and sight fishing; jigs, plugs, lures, dragging flies, and bait; fishing high, turbid waters; tying your own leaders; egg cures; gathering bait; do-it-yourself sinkers; hatchery and recycling programs; mounting your catch; cleaning and preparation; smoking your catch; and more. 6 x 9 inches, 135 pages.

SB: $15.95   **ISBN: 1-57188-295-2**

RECREATIONAL DUNGENESS CRABBING

By Scott Haugen

From Alaska to Mexico, Dungeness crabs are pursued for sport and their fine eating quality; Recreational Dungeness Crabbing gives you all the information you need to enjoy safe, fun, and productive crabbing. With an emphasis on family, safety, and fun, Haugen covers: natural history of the Dungeness crab; gear; bait; crabbing from a dock or boat; offshore crabbing; raking and dip netting; rod & reel; diving for crabs; crabbing in Oregon and Washington, including hot spots; cleaning and preparing your catch; favorite crab recipes; and more. 6 x 9 inches, 72 pages, full-color.

SB: $12.95   **ISBN: 1-57188-288-X**

EGG CURES
Proven Recipes & Techniques

By Scott Haugen

Of all the natural baits, many consider eggs to be the best. Before this book, you'd have an easier time getting the secret recipe for Coca-Cola than getting a fisherman to part with his personal egg cure. But now, Scott Haugen has done it for you, he went to the experts—fishermen and fishing guides—to get their favorite egg cures and fishing techniques, plus their secret tricks and tips. The result is this book. These 28 recipes come from anglers who catch fish—read this book and you will too. Guaranteed! 5 1/2 x 8 1/2 inches, 90 pages.

SB: $15.00   **ISBN: 1-57188-238-3**